Robert Hall Baynes

Home Songs for Quiet Hours

Robert Hall Baynes

Home Songs for Quiet Hours

ISBN/EAN: 9783741192203

Manufactured in Europe, USA, Canada, Australia, Japa

Cover: Foto ©Thomas Meinert / pixelio.de

Manufactured and distributed by brebook publishing software (www.brebook.com)

Robert Hall Baynes

Home Songs for Quiet Hours

HOME SONGS FOR QUIET HOURS.

NEW EDITIONS RECENTLY PUBLISHED.

LYRICS OF LOVE.

From Shakespeare to Tennyson.

Selected and arranged by W. Davenport Adams.   Price 2s. 6d.

"He has the prettiest love-songs for maids."—*Shakespeare.*

DEDICATED BY PERMISSION TO THE POET-LAUREATE.

SONGS FROM THE WORKS OF ALFRED TENNYSON.

Price 2s. 6d.

LONDON LYRICS.

By Frederick Locker.

Price 2s. 6d.

C. KEGAN PAUL AND CO., LONDON.

HOME SONGS

FOR QUIET HOURS.

EDITED BY

THE REV. R. H. BAYNES, M.A.,

HON. CANON OF WORCESTER AND VICAR OF ST. MICHAEL
AND ALL ANGELS, COVENTRY.

Editor of "*Lyra Anglicana*," "*English Lyrics*," "*Book
of Sacred Poetry*," "*Canterbury
Hymnal.*"

THIRD EDITION.

C. KEGAN PAUL AND CO., LONDON.
1878.

(All Rights reserved.)

✠

TO THE

BARONESS BURDETT-COUTTS,

IN GRATEFUL MEMORY OF MANY

KINDNESSES,

AND WITH HER LADYSHIP'S PERMISSION, THIS

COLLECTION OF SACRED POEMS

IS INSCRIBED.

✠

PREFACE.

 DO not feel that any apology is needed in sending forth another collection of Hymns and Sacred Songs for the help and solace of the various members of Christ's Church militant here on earth. It has ever been to me, in the midst of a very busy and responsible ministry, a source of exceeding gladness that I have been permitted, in any way, either to awaken or strengthen in earnest and thoughtful minds a sense of the value of really good Hymns, and their abiding influence on the heart and life. More than twelve years ago I ventured to write as follows :—

"It would be almost impossible to overrate the value of really good hymns for private as well as public use. Next to the Bible itself, hymns have done more to influence our views, and mould our theology, than any other instrumentality whatever. There is a power in hymns which never dies. Easily learned in the days of childhood and of youth; often repeated; seldom, if ever, forgotten; they abide with us, a most precious heritage amid all the changes of our earthly life. They form a fitting and most welcome expression for every kind of deep religious feeling; they are with us to speak of Faith and Hope in hours of trial and sorrow; with us to animate to all earnest Christian effort; with us as the rich consolation of individual hearts, and as one common bond of Fellowship between the living members of Christ's mystical Body."

And it is now some eight years since that, in the Preface to another collection, I thought fit to say that "there is a marvellous power of consolation and strength about true poetry, lighting up as it does, with its own special brightness, that which often seems to be material and common-place, and bringing home to us, in the way easiest of all to be remembered, the great lessons God would have us learn, amid the trials and discipline of our earthly life."

In simple illustration of these remarks, I may add that the "Lyra Anglicana" has had a sale of between forty and fifty thousand copies, and that the "English Lyrics," a book with which the great name of the ever-to-be-lamented Bishop Wilberforce was connected, is already out of print. I earnestly trust that the present Collection may carry on and deepen that blessed ministry of comfort and of strength which its predecessors have, by God's blessing, been permitted to fulfil. It only remains for me to acknowledge, with grateful thanks, the great kindness of friends and publishers in so freely allowing me the use of their respective copyrights. Among the former I must make especial mention of the Lord Bishop of Derry and Mrs. Alexander, C. L. Ford, Esq., Miss Hickey, Miss Doudney, and Miss Hayward; and among the latter, of Messrs. Houlston and Co., who have most courteously placed at my disposal some of the poems contributed to the "Churchman's Monthly Magazine" during the time of my editorship; of Messrs. Macmillan and Co., and of the Publishers of the "Leisure Hour."

R. H. B.

ADVENT, 1873.

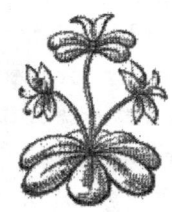

CONTENTS.

		Page
"The Life which I now live"	E. H. Hickey	1
The Waking Heart	B. M.	5
"In Memoriam"	W. Alexander, D.D., & C. F. Alexander	8
Hymn for Nightfall	W. Chatterton Dix	12
"She is not dead, but sleepeth"	C. L. Ford	14
A Dirge	G. J. Whyte-Melville	15
"Peace, be still"	William Leighton	17
Left Behind	E. H. Whiteman	19
Evening Hymn at Sea	Sarah Doudney	21
Aspirations		23
The Desire to Depart	B. M.	26
Night and Morning	A. J. Lymington	29
He is here	C. F. Alexander	31
Hymns for Confirmation	E. H. Hickey, & C. L. Ford	36
In Gethsemane	Augusta C. Hayward	39
Holy Communion	E. H. Hickey, & R. H. Baynes	41
"Entered in"	Gervase Robinson	48
In the Valley and Beyond it	A. S. Ormsby	50
The Easter Greeting	Augusta C. Hayward	53
Easter-Day	W. Chatterton Dix	55

Contents.

		Page
Questionings	C. L. Ford, B.A.	57
The Parish Priest	Author of "Vasco."	59
At Rest	E. H. Hickey	62
The Daily Communion	J. R.	66
On the Birth of Viscount Ednam	R. H. Baynes	70
Westward and Eastward	M. A. M.	71
Home!	Aug. C. Hayward	73
An Evening Prayer	M. L. B.	75
Good Friday	Rev. Herbert Todd	77
Death in the Fold		78
"Reprobate Silver"	C. L. Ford, B.A.	80
St. Michael's Victory		82
Hartlebury Castle	R. H. Baynes	85
"The Faithful in the Lord's Supper"		87
"Sit Anima mea cum ejus Anima!"	F. W. Harris, M.A.	89
Harvest Hymn	E. P.	91
"Blessed are the pure in heart"	E. H. Hickey	93
"That they All may be One"	E. H.	98
Poems from the Bible	A. Brodrick, B.A.	101
"Comfort ye"	E. Moultrie	104
Evening Hymn		106
Watching	Sarah Doudney	108
Home-Sickness	C. L. Ford, B.A.	111
Christmas	Frederick G. Lee	114
His Coming	A. C. Hayward	116
The Years that are Gone	A. C. Hayward	118
In Memory of Bishop Patteson	Sarah Doudney	120
Nothing but Leaves	Sarah Doudney	122

Contents.

		Page
Boaz Asleep	W. Alexander, D.D.	124
Christ and the Little Child	C. L. Ford, B.A.	127
A Vineyard Keeper		128
Eden	Rev. R. Winterbotham	131
A Carol for Christmas Eve	F. M. H.	135
Autumn	Ada Cambridge	139
Our Father in Heaven	W. Chatterton Dix	141
The Felled Tree	Sarah Doudney	144
"He will rest in His love"	Rev. H. L. Nicholson	146
The Wreck of the "Royal Charter"	C. F. Alexander	148
Not now	C. P.	152
What then?		154
Unrest		156
Rest in God	R. A. R.	157
Evening Hymn	A. A. Proctor	159
Vespers	C. M. P.	161
Heaven	N. A. W. Priest	162
"No more Sea"	C. F. M.	164
Waiting by the Gate	Wm. C. Bryant	169
Sunday Evening	W. M. Punshon	172
Twilight	Ada Cambridge	175
Night and Morning	W. Chatterton Dix	177
The Thorn in the Flesh	Ray Palmer	179
The Blood of Sprinkling	J. Guthrie	181
"In the Father's House"		182
In the Churchyard		184
"He Knoweth our Frame"	F. W. H. Myers	187
Waiting for Jesus	Sarah Doudney	189
American Missions	A. C. Coxe	191
In Lavington Churchyard	R. H. Baynes	193
Index of First Lines		195

HOME SONGS FOR QUIET HOURS.

"THE LIFE WHICH I NOW LIVE."

O, if a man should hear, all night, in dreaming,
    Music that lulls day's trouble into rest;
See, under closèd lids, the argent gleaming
    Of some sweet light wherein he deems him blest,

Would he not, all the live-long day, go longing
    For the fair blisses that the night renews?
Would he not watch the shadows in their thronging,
    Laugh for the dropping of the evening dews?

But, when a man has heard, in broad awaking,
    Music that strikes all meaner music dumb,
Seen, with unclosèd eyes, the glory breaking
    In the far East, because the Day has come,

Will not all things seem changed, and he, in patience,
  Swift-souled, yet hurrying not, pass on in grace,
Till the vast light of yearned-for revelations
  Smites him, elect, upon the lifted face?

What doth he reck of cedar or of brier?
  What doth he reck of glory or of shame?
Only he strains, with most extreme desire,
  Up to the God from Whom his calling came.

What doth he care if men should give or grudge him
  That vast belief that is indeed his due,
Seeing, O kith and kin, The Christ will judge him
  Nearer the naked soul of his than you?

Calm through the splendid heat of loyal passion,
  Fervid amid the judgment swift and clear,
Strong in the strength of self-renunciation
  Works he, and waits until the end appear.

Self trampled down by Love; so, for his choosing,
  On his life blazoned is the legend read;
In his superb young strength the angel bruising
  Under his holy feet the serpent's head.

Swift are his eyes to see; brighter, yet duller
  Than unto ours, to his anointed sight
Shows all the wild diversity of colour
  Passing into the harmony of light.

Swift are his ears to hear, how, deeply blending
  With the slow sobs of earth's extremest need,

"*The Life which I now live.*"

Rise stately notes of pæans high-ascending,
    Clashed out in triumph for the Conqueror's meed.

How was the glory won that folds around him?
    Did the strong soul indignant chafe and fret,
Panting to overleap the bounds that bound him,
    Those safe old barriers that our fathers set?

Or was it 'mid the wondrous incandescence
    Of the strong fire wherewith he was baptized,
Glad at his side he saw a glorious Presence,
    And by its love, he knew the Face of Christ?

Once of His laws, Whose life alone could reach them,
    Ay, and outshine the light wherein they wait,
Spake Jesus Christ, "Whoso shall do and teach them
    Shall in the kingdom be accounted great."

So we account this man, revering greatly
    One who could bear a life with love so fraught;
Even as the forest trees revere the stately
    Cedar that hears God's Voice, and breaketh not.

Seeketh he not to sit 'mid purple heather,
    Rivers and pastures calm beneath his feet,
Charmed by the birds of song and fairest feather,
    Round him an atmosphere of odour sweet;

Singeth he no love-songs for boys and maidens,
    Not for his path, as swift he passeth on,
Rhythmical shadows falling in sweet cadence,
    Chiming with delicate, slow lights anon!

"The Life which I now live."

Thrills his whole spirit with resistless tremor
    Under the lustral love's excessive might,
That ardent zone that, clasped by The Redeemer,
    Beats round his breast in waves of awful light.

Onward, with searching, eager eyes, unheeding
    Pain, nay nor death, so he may faithful prove—
Ravished because of loveliness exceeding,
    Captive because of agonizèd Love.

Ay, and yet more, in love that seems to borrow
    Strength from its yearning, he aspires to gain
That awful height of His sublimest sorrow
    Who was The King, thorn-crowned, of Love and Pain.

Yea, oh Thou Christ, he panteth, faileth for Thee,
    Pours his whole soul for chrism upon Thy Feet—
Unworthy, in Thy worthiness held worthy,
    Imperfect, in Thy perfectness complete.

E. H. Hickey.

THE WAKING HEART.

"I sleep, but my heart waketh."

IT is the Night; the lights are burning low,
    The house is still,
And through the heavy chambers come and go,
    At their own wayward will,
The Dreams that thrill the Night, with murmurings
Of voices, mingled with a rush of wings.

And going through the house, we are aware
    Of Dreams upon the wall,
Of Visions passing up the shadowy stair,
    And through the vacant hall;
And every sleeper, in his darkened room,
Is busy with his guests, in joy or gloom.

Ah! calm and still may be the sleeping face
    In the moonlight pale,
But the heart waketh in her secret place,
    Within the veil;
And agonies are suffered in the Night,
Or joys embraced, too keen for waking sight.

A cold wind blows out of the starry North,—
    Strange Doors stand wide,—

And hidden things, and things long past, come forth,
   And will not be denied,
Though some be terrible and sad to face,—
And the Heart mourneth, stricken, in her place.

But still she wakes; and, steadfast, will not turn
   To seek for rest;—
All the long Night her faithful Lamp will burn,
   In the clear breast,
Where Angels come and go, to minister
God's consolations, tenderly, to her.

Then come dear living ones across the Sea,
   From distant lands,—
Then come her Holy Dead, in ecstasy,
   With lilies in their hands,—
And looks, more sweet to these poor hearts of ours
Than even that fragrance of Eternal flowers!

And, dearer than the living ones, that dwell
   Beyond the throbbing Sea,—
And, dearer than the Dead, whose voices swell
   The Heavenly melody,—
ONE visiteth His people in the Night,
Who giveth songs, and makes the darkness bright.

"I sleep; yet evermore my Heart doth wake,
   Within the veil;
The voice of my Beloved! hear it break
   Across the moonlight pale:

He is come down to comfort me awhile,
And cheer the sad Night with His tender smile!"

* * * * *

And when the days and nights of Earth are flown,
    And I lie dead,
Then come and write, dear friends, upon the stone
    Above my quiet head,—
"I sleep;—yet far, upon the Crystal Sea,
    My Heart is waking,—waking, Lord, with
        Thee!"

For I shall sleep beneath the steadfast sky,
    So free from care,
That evermore my hands may folded lie,
    As if in prayer;
And evermore the sealèd eyelids keep
The secret of dim eyes, that, joyful, sleep:

And, whilst I sleep, behold! my Heart will wake,
    And sing its perfect song,
In Thy sweet Presence, Master, for whose sake
    It watched and waited long;
And evermore Thy deathless Love shall be
The treasure of the Heart that loveth Thee!

                              B. M.

"IN MEMORIAM"

SAMUEL WILBERFORCE, LATE BISHOP OF WINCHESTER, AT REST. JULY 18, MDCCCLXXIII.

OW thin the veil between our eyes,
    And angel wings in motion,
How narrow the long ledge that lies
    'Twixt us and death's dim ocean !

They rode by sunlit copse and glen
    And 'neath the woodland shadow,
They spurn'd with hoofs that rang again
    The cruel sloping meadow.

A plunge—a fall—and to the rock
    The veil was rent asunder;
How swift the change, how sharp the shock,
    How bright the waking yonder!

Old England heard it with a start,
    She mourns with voice uplifted—
Mother of many a noble heart,
    But ah! what Son so gifted?

From his own Oxford's storied hall
    Her stream by light oars ruffled,
To where beside the plane trees tall
    His Winton's bells are muffled.

"*In Memoriam.*"

The whole land wears the garb of grief
    For that great wealth departed,
Her peerless Prelate, Statesman, Chief,
    Large soul'd and gentle hearted.

The man so eloquent of word,
    Who sway'd all spirits near him,
Who did but touch the silver chord,
    And men perforce must hear him

Who won rude natures at his will,
    And charm'd them with the glamour
Of his sweet tongue; and kept them still
    Forgetful of their clamour.

Who from no task for Christ soe'er
    True soldier sought indulgence,
To him it wore so grand an air,
    Was lit with such effulgence.

Who sweetly smiled, and deftly plann'd,
    And his true work to fashion,
Like hammers in his skilful hand
    Took every party's passion.

Whom men call'd subtle overmuch
    Because all threads of beauty
He interwork'd, with magic touch,
    Into the web of duty.

And from their hundred varying dyes
    Wove well a wondrous colour,

That might have pleased malignant eyes
   More if it had been duller.

He for whom many hearts are sore,
   Lost to so many places,
The great Cathedral's crowded floor,
   A hush of upturn'd faces.

The village Church where children knelt
   Beneath his hands o'ershading,
And rugged men sweet comfort felt
   Or tender true upbraiding.

The Senate—barren evermore
   Of the rich voice that stirr'd it;
The platform, where the charm is o'er,
   That spell-bound all who heard it.

How many a noble deed he plann'd!
   How many a soul he guided,
With sympathy of heart and hand,
   And feelings many-sided!

And when the social lists were lit
   And worthy foeman tilted,
How flash'd the poniard of his wit,
   Keen-bladed!—diamond-hilted!

Sleep calm in earth—a Bishop robed
   Waiting God's golden morrow;—
O, memory leave the wound unprobed,
   Nor bring too sharp a sorrow!

Let love draw near and heav'n-born faith,
  Where the good Saint lies sleeping;
His white face beautiful in death,
  His soul in Christ's own keeping.

  W. ALEXANDER, D. D.,
   Bishop of Derry and Raphoe; and
  C. F. ALEXANDER.

HYMN FOR NIGHTFALL.

LIGHT the lamps, 'tis eventide,
Night falls fast on every side;
Now the prayers of saints arise,
Flame-like, to the darkening skies,
Whence, to welcome each appeal,
Soon the stars will softly steal.
                  Miserere Domine!

Has a sin its shadow cast
On the hours of labour past?
Let the prayer of penitence
Plead with Thee for each offence—
Plead till Thou dost all forgive,
Saying, "Turn again and live."
                  Miserere Domine!

Or if joy has cheered the day,
Gilding it with heavenly ray,
Now the blessed sun sinks down,
Peace will come that joy to crown;
Moon and stars light up the sky,
Peaceful angels hover nigh.
                  Miserere Domine!

Hymn for Nightfall.

This the prayer till partings o'er,
Till the sheep shall stray no more,
Till the silver piece be found,
And rejoicing spreads around,
As the endless Feast they keep,
Where they slumber not nor sleep:
    Miserere Domine!

Not on earth the quiet blest,
Where no strife disturbs their rest
Not on earth the day all bright,
Never fading into night;
Light and peace for evermore,
These upon the golden Shore:
    Gloria Tibi Domine!

    W. CHATTERTON DIX.

"SHE IS NOT DEAD, BUT SLEEPETH."

(*S. Luke* viii. 52.)

I.

"SHE is not dead!"
   Yet the wild funereal music fills the room,
   And wailing cries pierce through the outer
      gloom;
The hirelings laugh, and scorn Him to His face;
Yet still that stranger voice is heard,—" Give place !
   She is not dead, but sleepeth."

II.

"Weep not!" he saith;
Yet pale as June's first faded rosebud lies
The fair young girl before the Master's eyes;
Her bosom heaves no more with life's warm breath:
Yet still, "Why make ye this ado?" he saith:
   "She is not dead, but sleepeth."

III.

"She is not dead!"
Such the glad sound that wipes thy tears away,
O mourner, weeping for the fair lost clay
That crowned thy life with sweetness and with song—
Shall not the Master's voice be heard ere long?
   Then shall she wake who sleepeth.

C. L. FORD.

A DIRGE.

HILLS of heaven, bright and shining,
    Bid thee welcome ! Spirits wait,
Thronging down to greet thee, twining
    Garlands at the golden gate !
See ! before thee flash and quiver,
    Rising in eternal light,
Daybreak on the crystal river,
    And behind thee, night !
Earth hath been wearing thee, now it is past ;
    Providence sparing thee,
    Mercy preparing thee,
Angels are bearing thee Homeward at last !

    Quenched the bitter taste of sorrow,
        Quelled the angry throb of pain,
    Glad, yet fearless of the morrow,
        Thine the bliss without the bane.
    Done with earthly trouble, taking
        Thought no more for earthly care,
    Spent with earthly travail, waking
        For its wages there !
Earth hath been wearing thee, now it is past ;
    Providence sparing thee,
    Mercy preparing thee,
Angels are bearing thee Homeward at last !

A Dirge.

Songs of heaven triumphant singing,
    Rank on rank, in waves of light,
March the immortal legions, bringing
    Crowns of gold and robes of white;
Far above thee, lustre streaming
    Round its towers unbuilt by hands,
Through a mist of glory beaming,
    See, the City stands!
Earth hath been wearing thee, now it is past;
    Providence sparing thee,
    Mercy preparing thee,
Angels are bearing thee Homeward at last!

                G. J. WHYTE-MELVILLE.

"PEACE, BE STILL."

WHEN the clouds loom dark and eerie,
    And the heavens are fraught with ill,
Flesh is weak and heart is weary,
    Saviour, whisper, " Peace, be still."

When the mighty storm is surging,
    Stars are hid, and winds are shrill,
Satan striving, passion urging,
    Saviour, whisper, " Peace, be still."

When the waves of doubt and terror
    Toss me at their own wild will;
Light seems dark, and truth seems error,—
    Saviour, whisper, " Peace, be still."

When affliction's storms are howling,
    And its voice my soul doth thrill;
Earth is black, and heaven is scowling,—
    Saviour, whisper, " Peace, be still."

When the shadows round me thicken,
    Bitter tears mine eyelids fill,
Spirit faints and senses sicken,—
    Saviour, whisper, " Peace, be still."

"Peace, be still."

When the tide of death's cold river
   Shocks me with its icy chill,
Body quakes and billows quiver,—
   Saviour, whisper, " Peace, be still."

WILLIAM LEIGHTON.

LEFT BEHIND.

WE whisper, "It is over now for thee,"
    Standing in presence of the holy dead
Over the pain we long have wept to see,
    Over the struggle dread.

Over the wistful looking back to life,
    The daily haunting of the word, Farewell,
The secret woe of flesh and soul at strife
    No utterance might tell.

Over the speechless heavenward appeal,
    When past and future urge their strange alarms,
And the faint soul must lower sink to feel
    The Everlasting Arms.

Over for us, alas! upon the stair
    No more we hear their footsteps come and go,
No more their voices, when we meet in prayer,
    Accordant, sweet and low.

No more their beauty-loving eye discerns
    The green wheat springing in the fields afar.
The haunt of purple briony, or ferns,
    The first pale evening star.

No more their magic memory wakes to words,
   Poems, and legends heard in bygone days,
And caught upon the wing like singing birds,
   Or snatched like hedgerow sprays.

No more their eyes light up to meet our joy,
   Nor their caressing hands allay our pain,
And chase the petty torments that annoy
   Our busy heart and brain.

No more they make their life's experience ours,
   To keep like jewels they have won and worn,
Saying, " Here grew the wheat and here the flowers,
   Here lies a hidden thorn."

Over ! No more ! Oh, words, for us ye strike
   The key-note of bereavement's funeral song,
Which, high or low, all voices sing alike
   In solemn choral song.

Over ! No more ! Oh, words, for them ye sound
   The key-note of a calm triumphal hymn,
Where voices of the angels are not found
   Nor heaven-born seraphim.

A song for those that, safe from sin and loss,
   Beyond the sea are resting on the shore—
Who 'neath the crown look backward to the cross :
   Over ! No more ! No more !

E. H. WHITEMAN.

EVENING HYMN AT SEA.

"Then they that were in the ship came and worshipped Him."

E come to Thee, sweet Saviour, humbly
    seeking
  Thy shelter when the darkness draweth
    nigh;
Fain would our listening spirits hear Thee speaking;
  Be with us, Lord, and whisper, "It is I."

Comfort Thy weary ones, whose hearts are bending
  Beneath the burdens of this world of care;
Show them in dreams "the life that hath no ending,"
  And tell them of the joy that waits them there.

Hold all our dear ones safely in Thy keeping,
  Give them bright thoughts of Thee and tranquil
    rest;
Shine on the far-off homes where they are sleeping,
  Bless them, sweet Saviour, and they shall be blest!

If there be tears on some beloved faces,
  Smile on them, Jesus, chase their grief away;
O bid Thine angels fill our vacant places,
  Watching the friends we love by night and day.

EVENING HYMN AT SEA.

" Then they that were in the ship came and worshipped Him."

WE come to Thee, sweet Saviour, humbly
    seeking
      Thy shelter when the darkness draweth
        nigh ;
Fain would our listening spirits hear Thee speaking ;
    Be with us, Lord, and whisper, " It is I."

Comfort Thy weary ones, whose hearts are bending
    Beneath the burdens of this world of care ;
Show them in dreams " the life that hath no ending,"
    And tell them of the joy that waits them there.

Hold all our dear ones safely in Thy keeping,
    Give them bright thoughts of Thee and tranquil
      rest ;
        the far-off homes where they are sleeping,
            and they shall be blest !

Evening Hymn at Sea.

A word of Thine can still the troubled ocean,
   Thy Spirit moves upon the pathless deep;
We lift our prayers to Thee in meek devotion,
   And, guarded by Thy mercy, softly sleep.

Oh! by Thy Name upon our hearts engraven,
   And by the blood that bought our souls for Thee,
Bring us at last unto that blessed haven
   Where there is no more night and no more sea!
                        Amen.
                    SARAH DOUDNEY.

ASPIRATIONS.

AH, Lord! to be
    The least of all that wait on Thee :
      To stand as one
    Whose loins are girt with power to run
  The appointed race,
Upheld by meekness, truth, and grace ;
    To whom, beside,
All else with Christ is crucified,
    And loss is gain ;
To whom Thy love is Peace in pain,
    As one who hears—
Beyond the tumult of the years,
    The strife, the sin,
The tribulation, toil, and tears,—
    Thy words of mercy, " Enter in ! "

Ah, Lord ! that I may be
This chosen vessel meet for Thee,—
    That I, so poor,
May joy o'er Thy great wealth in store ;
That I, so frail, weak,—utterly,—
May strengthened be of Thine and Thee ;
    That I, so vile,
May yet rejoice me in the smile
Of Him who died the death for me ;—

That I indeed may feel
The Lord my passionate appeal
    Will hear;
And in His own good time make clear
Of these my torments, Doubt and Fear.

    But what am I
To stand without and call and cry?
    Behold, I plead,
In this mine hour of utmost need,
The unimaginable pain
Of Him, the guiltless, scourged and slain
    For me.
O Lamb of God! mine eyes to Thee
    I lift, as one
Who watcheth for the morning sun;—
    In mercy visit me!

    I stand awhile
To view, beneath, the dim defile,
    Through which the Lord my doubtful way
    Hath wrought from darkness into day:
And shall I falter here?
    I stand before
    The temple door,
And wait until my Lord appear.

For this I surely know:
The grace of Jesu hitherto,
    Alone, hath kept
    Me in the dark where conscience slept;

And straight and plain
Through all the past, or peace or pain,
I mark and prove
The guiding of the Lord of Love.

Lord Jesu! grant me grace
And meekness in Thy Holy Place;
    A spirit fine
To cleave the gross, and calm resign
My very life, if life it be,
That separates my soul and Thee.

THE DESIRE TO DEPART.

"Hadad said unto Pharaoh, Let me depart, that I may go to mine own country. Then Pharaoh said unto him, But what hast thou lacked with me, that, behold, thou seekest to go to thine own country? And he answered, Nothing: howbeit let me go in any wise."

1 Kings xi. 21, 22.

AND thus our hearts appeal to them,
   When we behold our dearest rise,
And look towards Jerusalem
   With strangely kindling eyes.

And thus we vainly seek to hide
   With the poor curtain of our love
The shining Gates that open wide,
   To welcome our sweet saints above.

Yet still to them, from that bright Land,
   Through our thin tent the Glory gleams;
Already lost to us they stand
   Wrapp'd in a mist of golden dreams:

For ah! the Master is so fair,
   His smile so sweet to banish'd men,
That they who meet it unaware
   Can never rest on Earth again.

And they who see Him risen afar
   At God's right hand to welcome them,
Forgetful stand of home and land,
   Desiring fair Jerusalem.

Yet had we lavish'd at their feet
  The precious ointment of hearts that break
For love; we counted sorrow sweet,
  And pain a crown for their dear sake :

" What have ye lack'd, beloved, with us,"
  We murmur heavily and low,
"That ye should rise with kindling eyes,
  And be so fain to go ?"

And tenderly the answer falls
  From lips that wear the smile of Heaven :
" Dear ones," they say, " we pass this day
  To Him by whom your love was given ;

And in His Presence clear and true,
  We answer you with hearts that glow,—
No good thing have we lack'd with you—
  Howbeit, let us go !"

And even as they speak, their thoughts
  Are wandering upward to the Throne.
Ah ! God, we see, at length, how free
  All earthly ties must leave Thine own.

Yet, kneeling low in darken'd homes,
  And weeping for the treasure spent,
We bless Thee, Lord, for that sweet word
  Our dear ones murmur'd as they went,—

It was not that our love was cold,
  That earthly lights were burning dim,

But that the Shepherd from His Fold
   Had smiled, and drawn them unto Him :

Praise God the Shepherd is so sweet !
   Praise God the Country is so fair !—
We could not hold them from His feet,—
   We can but haste to meet them There.

B. M.

NIGHT AND MORNING.

LORD! in love and mercy save us,
    For our trust is all in Thee;
In that cleansing fountain lave us,
    Which alone can make us free!

"Weary, life's rough billows breasting,
    Through the long, lone, dismal night;
Grant that, calmly on Thee resting,
    We may wait for morning light;

"When the sun shall shine forth, bringing
    Peace, with healing on his wings,
And—all sadness changed to singing—
    Thirst be slaked in living springs.

"Lord! we pray, and know Thou hearest,
    For Thy promises are true;
Grant the heart-wish that is dearest,—
    He who knows can also do!

"What though night-black storms of sorrow,
    Chafing, blind our eyes with tears?
Joy, we know, comes with the morrow,
    For our heavenly Father hears;—

"Hears, and shall not more or longer
  Try us than our strength can bear—
Lift the cross, or make us stronger;—
  Trust all to His loving care!

"Change, O Lord!—we pray in meekness—
  Israel's wail to Miriam's song:
Feeling our own utter weakness,
  Let us in Thy strength be strong!"

A. J. LYMINGTON.

HE IS HERE.

(Written for the "Church of Ireland Parochial Magazine.")

DREAM'D a dream while, piping low,
    The wind did blow into the West,
And a great tide came surging slow
    Up broad Lough Swilly's heaving breast.

From cliffs, and many archèd caves,
    To touch her inland trees and meadows,
Came up the salt Atlantic wave—
    "Is this our lake of many shadows?

"There's not a light on isle or bay,
    The hills are wrapt as if for thunder,
The sky above is leaden grey,
    Like darker lead the waters under."

The mist came down and held the plain,
    It was a dreary hour, that seem'd
Attuned to thoughts of gloom and pain;
    I lay, and as I look'd, I dream'd.

Out of the highways and the hedges
    Methought a ghastly crowd had met,
Brown hands that seek to grasp the edges
    Of that calm throne where we are set.

The calm of culture, too refined
    For those lost creatures, whom the world
Plays with awhile, then drops behind,
    From depth to depth of ruin whirl'd.

Twice fallen souls, who fell with Eve,
    And fall again by choice of sin,
Who break themselves the pale, and leave
    The fold where Christ had penn'd them in.

Some wan, some haggard, some still fair—
    Sad beauty in a sullied shrine—
The mask above the hard despair,
    The heart that aches, the eyes that shine.

Methought that in their midst did rise
    A Preacher with God's blessed Book.
Kind words he pleaded, pure and wise,
    Love in his heart and in his look.

Words tenderer, truer, wiser, there;
    For that he brought to that foul place
From his own home a purer air,
    A brightness from his wife's sweet face.

He told of love that died for hate,
    How sin corrupts, and then destroys.
He show'd the open golden Gate,
    And sang them of celestial joys.

In vain, in vain—no voice, no moan—
    The wind did blow into the West;

He is here.

The sky was lead, the hearts were stone,
   No sunbeam lit the gulf's dark crest.

Then did a charm of colour'd light—
   A sudden gleam—the hills suffuse,
They stood transfigured to my sight,
   A mass of delicate lilac hues.

The waves beneath ran green and blue,
   Rose-tinctured where the last cloud lay;
God's blessed sun had broken through,
   God's light was lovely on the bay.

O beautiful salt, sunlit lake,
   Whose waters welter to my feet,
Is there no moral charm to make
   That other darkness bright and sweet?

Still I dream'd on, and heard the prayer
   From the Priest's lips; and saw the storm
In lurid eyes, and was aware
   Suddenly of another form.

A thousand painters' hands have tried,
   And with a touch almost divine,
To give again that wounded Side,
   The Hands, the Feet, the Eyes' calm shine.

But not the most angelic touch
   That ever bade the canvas glow,
Gave form, or face, or beauty, such
   As on my ravish'd sight did grow.

He show'd His hands, He show'd the wound,
  He look'd in love on that wild horde,
A gesture pleading without sound,
  And eyes that spake without a word.

Methought out of the crowd He took
  A woman's hand; and in the bold,
Hard depths of her seared eyes did look
  Reproachful pity: so of old

He look'd on him, the thrice forgiven,
  Till he went out, and wept his fall;
So sent he forth the woman shriven,
  Who gave for love her best and all.

Then spake the Preacher, "This is He,
  The Christ of God, the Lord from Heaven."
Ah! then the sunlight touch'd the sea,
  The springs leap'd up, the stone was riven.

There was a burst of broken sighs,
  A sound of lips that strove to pray,
And penitent tears, and groans, and cries
  For pardon, as He pass'd away.

O Preachers on a desolate coast,
  That call to souls, and call in vain—
The women in the highways lost,
  The men that sin, and sin again—

Show them, to kindle pure desire,
  How "One like to the Son of Man"

Is walking with them through the fire,
　Is sitting with the publican.

Tell them He comes in showers of grace,
　Tell them He comes with Wine and Bread,
When Eucharistic feasts have place,
　When Whitsun skies are overhead.

And still the harp no comfort brings,
　And still the soul is unsufficed,
Without the charm that breaks the springs,
　The Presence of the living Christ.

C. F. ALEXANDER.

HYMNS FOR CONFIRMATION.

I.

OH Christ, My God, to Thee I once arose
    From the fair tide o'er which thy Dove
        did brood,
    Bathed in the splendour of the Easter
        glows,
Clad in Thy gracious favour's amplitude.

Oh, Saviour sweet, mine holy Chrysome caught
    The marring dust of earth, and was defiled;
Yet to thy breast in pity Thou hast brought
    Loved back to purity Thy sinning child.

Here, with bared brow, whereon Thy loving eye
    Sees Thine own Cross gleam faint through mists of
        sin,
Lift I the prayer, made strong exceedingly;
    Now let thy child Thy glorious likeness win.

Here, Lord, I vow the fight perpetual,
    Taking no rest until the day may be
When sin and doubt, that fain would slay me, shall
    Be drown'd for ever in life's waveless sea.

Here, oh! my Captain, pour Thy life in mine,
　　The Blood of Thy new Testament, and give
The Bread that I desire perpetually,
　　The Bread whereby Thy children's souls shall live.

Tis done, Thy Holy Church hath set Thy seal
　　Upon my head, and crown'd its locks with grace;
Now, oh! my Saviour, at Thy feet I kneel,
　　Hereafter Thou wilt let me see Thy face.

E. H. HICKEY.

II.

LORD! from this time we cry to Thee,
Thou of our youth the guide shalt be!
Draw near, and take us by the hand,
And lead into the upright land!
With fire by night, with cloud by day,
Be with us in our pilgrim way.

Forth to the wilderness we go,
The tempter's wiles ordain'd to know:
Though weak our arm, and fierce the fight,
Still may we conquer through Thy might!
Till, every foul assault subdued,
Our souls are fed with angels' food.

In sorrow's cloud, in trouble's sea,
Baptized afresh, O Lord, to Thee,

While every joy that round us springs
A Eucharistic gladness brings,
Each journey done, each danger past,
Receive us to Thy rest at last.

Uphold our footsteps in Thy way,
Nor suffer us in heart to stray:
With patience bear, with counsel guide,
From follies wean, from perils hide;
In suffering soothe, in want defend;
Confirm and 'stablish to the end!

C. L. Ford.

IN GETHSEMANE.

"LET Thy Will be done!" One prayed,
Kneeling in the olive shade,
Through the Paschal pale moonlight,
Through the sadness of the night;
Through the river's murmur deep,
Through the sleeper's wearied sleep,
Fell the words, "Thy will be done!"
Rose His prayer Who pray'd alone
        In Gethsemane.

Hush'd and soft the prayer-words fell
Through the strife inaudible,
While the centuries of crime
Darken'd round that hour of time;
And the spirit powers drew nigh
To the sin-bought victory,—
And for man, but One, but One,
Praying, "Let Thy Will be done!"
        In Gethsemane.

It was done! For Him the day
Dawning on the Dolorous Way,
Closing of the Heavenly Place,
Hiding of the Father's Face;

And the Cross on Calvary,
And the death that mortals die;
But for us the Victor's tone,
Saying, " Let Thy Will be done ! "
                In Gethsemane.

Wide the words re-echo still,
Spreading from that olive hill,
Hush'd and soft the voices come,
Through the Church's world-stretch'd Home,
" Let Thy Will be done ! "—the cry
Of the saving Agony;
And the thankful Antiphon,
" Father ! Father ! it is done ! "
                In Gethsemane.

" Be it done ! " we say it here;
In its meaning new and dear
Sounds no more of Sacrifice,
Guides to rest in Paradise.
" It is done ! " and thus we come,
Gathering to the Father's Home,
Living, dying, lost not one,
Perfected the Prayer begun
                In Gethsemane.

              AUGUSTA C. HAYWARD.

HOLY COMMUNION.

I.

BEAUTIFUL comforting words,
   Ye travailing, come unto me,—
Come now, for the Vine is our Risen
      Lord's,
Who calleth us here to be
Made one with Him, as His grace accords
   In this Holiest Mystery.

Here, O our Saviour sweet,
   Will we seek Thy unveil'd face;
Approach with the tread of welcome feet
   To the loveliness of the place
Where the Bridegroom stoops His bride to greet
   With the jewels of His grace.

O by Thy sacrifice
   Once made for the sinner's sake,
Look on each heart that before Thee lies,
   The strength of its earth-bonds break.
Thou, the All-Loving, All-True, All-Wise,
   We take Thee—do Thou us take.

O strength for the working-days!
   O Light in the path we tread!

O echoes sweet of the burst of praise
    That uprose when we banqueted
With the King of Kings in the Holy Place,
    Where His Son, our Brother, led.

But alas! how few are here—
    For the many have scorn'd the Board,
And turn'd away with unheeding ear
    From the voice of their God and Lord.—
Yet a little longer, O Saviour dear,
    Let them hear Thy gracious word!

With lips all parched and dried
    For unhallow'd food of swine,
And the terror of thirst unsatisfied,
    For the world-draught dash'd with brine,
They turn'd from the Bread of Life aside,
    And drank not the King's own Wine.

O weep who deny Him to-day!
    Ere another week may be,
And the Banquet again be spread, ye may
    In the dark go forth,—what if HE
Here present in yearning love, should say
    In His wrath, "Depart from me?"

II.

AH spear-torn Heart, dear place to hide
　　Me in Thou art; and here, I say,
　　The world can never take away
Thy peace from me, Lord, who hast died
　　And risen again, that I might be
　　Brought into covenant with Thee.

Among ten thousand chiefest Thou,
　　Thy vesture white of stately fold,
　　And zoned Thy breast with ardent gold,
And as the strong sun shineth now
　　Thy Face, once marr'd; and Thou hast laid
　　Thy hand on me—"Be not afraid!

"Mine amaranthal robe is thine,
　　And God the Father, pleased doth see
　　Each one of Mine complete in Me;
And thou shalt in My kingdom shine
　　For evermore." Oh, Jesus Christ,
　　I eat and drink, and am sufficed!

"Yet more—ere dawn that glorious day
　　I will come down thy work to see;
　　And when thy lilies full-blown be,
Well-pleased will gather many a spray,
　　For the Bride's locks a wreath to twine
　　Of fair white thoughts and deeds of thine."

My King! I praise Thee for the gift
  Wherewith it is Thy will to bless
  Me, who am all unworthiness;
The beggar up from shame to lift,
  And put Thy raiment clean on me,
  That men may know me loved of Thee!

Thou makest me to love Thee! yes,
  Thou Saviour sweet, of me denied,
  Who didst to me turn, loving-eyed,
With that deep look, and then didst bless
  The penitential tears I shed,
  And madest me be comforted.

Unworthy e'en to gather up
  The crumbs beneath Thy table, Thou
  Givest Thy Flesh to feed me now,
And in Thy covenantal Cup
  Quenchest the thirsting agony
  Of the parch'd lips that fail'd for Thee!

                E. H. HICKEY.

III.

THOU, Who on Calvary's Tree,
  The awful Cross for me
  In anguish deep and bitter pain didst bear,
  Look down in pity sweet,
    O Saviour! make me meet
The Chalice of Thy suffering to share!

Holy Communion.

I need Thy strength Divine
To nerve this heart of mine,
So that I shrink not from the daily Cross
Thy tender love dost send
To keep me to the end,
Counting for Thy dear sake all else but dross.

Most frail am I, and weak,
And scarcely dare to speak
Of all my sins and sorrows, Lord, to Thee.
Yet Thou for me hast died,
I see Thy wounded Side,
Thy Blood-stain'd Brow,—and this is all my plea.

Lord Christ I Thee adore
And long to love Thee more,
And serve Thee better 'midst this earthly strife;
Make me more earnest, true,
Help me Thy work to do,
Ere the night cometh, O Thou Light of Life!

Here on Thine altar stair,
I kneel in faith and prayer,
Pour wine of Heaven upon my parchèd lip;
Now, with the living Bread
O let my soul be fed,
And nourish'd in Thy Church's fellowship!

Then when the fight is fought,
Me, whom Thy love hath bought,

Bring safely Home where all Thy glories shine;
    To see Thee face to face,
    To rest in Thy embrace,
And in Thy kingdom drink the endless Wine!

R. H. BAYNES.

IV.

JESUS, thou true and living Bread,
    Sent down from Heaven our hearts to cheer,
Thy Feast of wondrous Love is spread,
    And, all unworthy, we draw near.

We come, for Thou Thyself dost call
    And words of endless comfort speak,
Low at Thy wounded Feet we fall,
    And pardon through Thy Blood we seek.

Helpless to Thy dear Cross we cling,
    On Thee our sins and sorrows lay,
Our weary souls to Thee we bring,
    O touch and cleanse them all to-day

When foes are round us like a flood,
    Uphold us in the bitter strife,
Thy Body and Thy precious Blood
    Preserve to everlasting life.

Holy Communion.

Make now Thy nearest Presence known
   In this Thy Feast of Love Divine,
And hearts that long for Thee alone,
   Fill with the Cup of Heavenly Wine.

Father! accept for Jesus' sake,
   Our sacrifice of praise and prayer;
Like unto Him Thy children make,
   Until the Crown of Life we wear.

R. H. BAYNES.

"ENTERED IN."

DEAD but a moment! and my Daughter's
    kiss
      Yet living on my cheek;
  Dead but a moment! and the Heavens
of bliss
    Upon my vision break;

"Dead but a moment! and the saintly walls
    Agleam with jewell'd gates;
The tone of music as from inner halls;
    YON FACE which foremost waits!

"Smiling as when at death we stood to part
    In the far-faded past;
Dear One, how changed thou art, how new thou
      art,
    Since I beheld thee last!

"I saw thee then; thou hadst thy shroud about
    thee;
    Adieu to me and breath.
And after came the desolate years without thee,
    And last my own poor death.

"And now it seems as yesterday the whole,
    The bliss, the pang, the tears:

And I have touched thee once again where roll
  The shadows of no years.

" How fresh thou art, dear One ; how strong and
    new !
  How pure and holy now !
The incorruptible within, the dew
  Of youth upon thy brow !

" And what a land is this ! what bowers ! what hills !
  And what a river floweth !
What bands who follow Him through golden stills
  Whithersoe'er He goeth !

 " Lead me to Him the first, whose love and grace
    Made that rude earth seem sweet :
Lead me to Him that I may see His face,
  That I may kiss His feet."

GERVASE ROBINSON.

IN THE VALLEY AND BEYOND IT.

(Psalm xxiii. *Rev.* xxi.)

THEY are going—ever going—through this
    pilgrim land below,
Like the wind's unceasing murmur, or the
    river's ceaseless flow;
Through the valley of the Shadow—to the Border
    Land they go.

They are going—ever going—some are walking
    quickly by,
With their hopes on Jesus centred, and a bright
    uplifted eye,
To the mountain peaks appearing in the glowing
    evening sky !

They are going—ever going—some are lingering,
    half afraid,
As they near the foaming river, which is in the
    darkest shade;
All the burden of their lifetime seems upon them
    freshly laid.

They are going—ever going—some a ransomed, happy band,
With crowns of gold upon each head, and palms within each hand,
Bright with rays of distant glory from the bright Celestial Land!

They are going—ever going—as they near the dark stream's side
God's own promises about it, brighten e'en its leaden tide,
And they calmly pass throughout it, and they join the glorified!

Pass they onward, ever calmly, for the staff of One is there
Who will guide them through its waters, will their fainting souls upbear,
Till they reach the land beyond them where they'll all His glory share.

And in joy, all unimagined, they for aye and aye will reign,
Free from every doubt and sorrow, free from every care and pain;
And they'll look back o'er their pilgrimage, and see each loss was gain!

Now they reap the golden Harvest of the seeds in sadness sown,

They have pass'd through life's "deep waters," and
    through sorrows all unknown—
And they join the Alleluias of the ransomed round
    the Throne!

And that glorious psalm is singing, all so wondrous
    and so sweet;
And afar its music ringing echoes throughout the
    golden street,
Where the saved ones are flinging all their Crowns
    at Jesus' feet!

A. S. ORMSBY.

THE EASTER GREETING

(FROM THE GERMAN OF KARL GEROK.)

WHY weepest thou?—to Mary Magdalen
    Came the first joy of resurrection-
        greeting:
    Still, through the gloom of tears and
grief, again
We hear that voice, the Easter words repeating;
    Why weepest thou?

Why weepest thou?—unknown, yet still the same,
    The Heavenly Gardener, bearing flowers im-
        mortal,
Beside thee stands, to call thee by thy name,
    And point to Eden's ever-open portal;—
    Why weepest thou?

Why weepest thou?—is the departed Lord
    By wrong and judgment from thy presence taken?
Look up—behold Him! by the grave restored,
    In Godlike power from death's short night to
        waken;—
    Why weepest thou?

Why weepest thou?—is there a load of sin
  That seals the sepulchre with weight oppressing?
Only thy dead transgression lies within;
  Without, thy Lord draws near with pard'ning
      blessing;—
        Why weepest thou?

Why weepest thou?—is it that earthly care
  Darkens thy life with tempest-clouds of sorrow?
Look up, behold, in Heaven how pure and fair,
  Dawns on the night of death the Easter morrow;—
        Why weepest thou?

Why weepest thou?—over the long-mourn'd dead?
  Only the mortal part with earth is blended,
Far from the tomb, in paths where Jesus led,
  Homeward the spirit has to God ascended;—
        Why weepest thou?

Why weepest thou?—in the long journey's gloom
  Do the slow years delay thy heav'nward yearning?
Lo! He awaits thee in the Father's Home,
  There worn feet rest, from pilgrim toil returning;—
        Why weepest thou?

Why weepest thou?—Lord, Thou hast given each
      day
  Some drops of joy in every cup of sadness;
Soon Thou wilt wipe all tears of grief away,
  There, where Heaven's songs repeat the words of
      gladness,
        Why weepest thou?

AUGUSTA C. HAYWARD.

EASTER-DAY.

SEPULCHRED and wave-wash'd dead,
    Sleepers where no mortal tread
    Breaks the silence of your rest,
    Deep in gorge, on mountain's crest;
There is news for you to-day,
Christ the King hath been your way,
In His beauty past compare,
Lord of life and Victor fair:
He whose garment is the Light,
He whose strong right Hand of might
Shatter'd hell and burst its bars,
Glorious in His wounds and scars:
Fresh from conflict with the foe,
Red in His apparel's glow,
Fresh from conquest won alone,
Won for ever for His own.
Through the city's gloom He went,
Where the living are content,
For the greed of gain, to sell
Bodies He redeem'd so well:
Through the yards of nameless graves,
He who the forgotten saves.

Through the long Cathedral aisle,
Where the fitful sunbeams smile,

As they seem in sport to pass
Through the many-tinted glass:
And He mark'd the sleepers there,
Priest and noble, young and fair,
And the babe, whose mother's breast
But a moment gave it rest.
Through the village Churchyard, too,
While the graves were bright with dew,
Where the snowdrop hangs her head,
Primroses their fragrance shed,
And the birds their matins wake
Soon as day begins to break.

Over many a corpse-sown flood,
Over plains once red with blood,
Through the haunts where guilt holds breath
Pass'd the Lord of Life and Death,
With His banners all unfurl'd,
Come with healing for the world,
He, the Victor in the strife,
Resurrection and the Life!

Yes, my King, the dead upraise Thee,
They gone down to silence praise Thee,
And the living service pay,
Quick and dead at one to-day,
Call'd the Paschal Feast to share:
O that we all keep it There,
Where nor death nor night is known,
Round about Thy Glory-Throne.

W. CHATTERTON DIX.

QUESTIONINGS.

"Then I said in my heart, that this also is vanity."—Eccles. ii. 15.

HAT is life, but sowing,
    Sowing on the sand?
What is death but going
    To a fog-bound land?
What is love, but burning
    Of a useless fire?
What is hope, but learning,
    Limit of desire?

Yet, if life were sowing
    Of a hopeful seed,
Then might death be growing
    Up to life indeed.
Then might love be burning
    Of a quenchless fire;
Then might hope be learning
    Fulness of desire.

Life is nought but dying—
    Love alone is life;
Love is endless sighing—
    Hope is aimless strife.

Yet, O doubting lisper,
  Hear a voice which saith,
In most hopeful whisper,
  " Love's true life is death."

    CHARLES LAWRENCE FORD, B. A.

THE PARISH PRIEST.

ID darkest haunts of sin,
   A veteran warrior, steadfast, undeterr'd,
   With holy pitying love his bosom stirr'd,
     Stands forth, and enters in.

   God's light upon his brow,
Divine compassion in his earnest eyes,
Making the sin-bound sufferers arise,
     And hope—they know not how.

   Grief in his sadden'd tones—
Earth's shadows veiling immortality;
His woe—to see his brethren sin and die;
     His anguish—brethren's groans.

   He meets a cold world's scorn;
Heeds not the slander and the mockery,—
Learning to wear in felt serenity
     The robe his Lord hath worn.

   The angels gaze below,
And watch him as he passes on his way;
Their smiles fall, as some fair celestial ray,
     Upon his lowly brow.

The spirits of the dead
Hover around him in his darkest hours,
Putting to flight the host of rebel powers
    By the great tempter led.

    He treads affliction's briars;
His tender heart is school'd to suffer here;
Yet knows it not one touch of craven fear;
    His Master's strength inspires.

    The staff of life is prayer;
The breath of life is love and holiness;
Loving and praying—living but to bless,
    He calm abideth there;

    Waiting his glorious call,
When loosed from earth his spirit shall arise
To share eternal light, and from his eyes
    The darkening scales shall fall.

    Oh triumph of the soul!
Rich victory achieved o'er hostile power;
Each sigh that rends thy heart—each suff'ring hour,
    Brightens thy aureole.

    For time shall cease to be;
All that now weighs thy lot shall pass away,
And but the mem'ry of thy warfare stay
    To bless eternity.

    As the tired warrior rests,
After the " din of arms and battle roar,"

So shalt thou rest upon the stilly shore
    Amid the marriage guests.

And we who view thee now,
Enshrine in memory thy holy strife,
And watch thee to the portal of that life
    Which all who "love" shall know.

Thy track remains in sight—
A silver cord over the waters drawn,
Leading us through the dark; that, at the dawn,
    We too may wake in light.

THE AUTHOR OF "VASCO."

AT REST.

HANK God that Gerizim's sweet dews have
    Cool'd my parch'd forehead's fierce fever;
That Ebal's strong anguish and awe have
    Pass'd from my spirit for ever.
Bless God, Oh my soul, for the love
    Whose Author and Giver hath sent thee,
The Comforter's presence, instead of the
    Thirsted-for draught of Nepenthe.

The passion of striving is o'er, and I take
    The free gift He has given
With the faith of a child, and of such, saith
    Christ, is the kingdom of Heaven.
And the rags of my tatter'd resolves are cast
    Off, for His love has put on me
A robe of desire that is pledge of the
    Kingdom His passion has won me.

O Saviour, I kneel at Thy feet: Thou
    Hast said none shall ever be sent thence;
I wipe with the locks of submission—
    I wash'd with the tears of repentance;

At Rest.

And the spirit made whole by Thy word,
   In the radiance and rapture adoreth,
Till the whole place be fill'd with the breath
   Of the odorous nard it outpoureth.

Love and truth met with faces unveil'd in
   The Rest that was lit with His presence,
Led up the high mount of Delight, whose
   Glory can know no senescence,
And the mist has roll'd off and for aye,
   And not in mere vision come o'er me,
Large gleamings of Light from the place
   Where the City of God has her glory.

O Light, who art love! O Love, who art Christ!
   Thou wouldst never abandon,
That seeing I might not perceive, and hearing
   Have no understanding.
O Sculptor Divine, Thou alone with Thy
   Mystical chisel couldst fashion
For the rigid acceptance of fate Thy
   Beautiful grace Resignation.

Lord, what wouldst Thou have me do? I wait
   But to know what Thy will is;
Come down, O my King, to my heart, and
   Gather thence odorous lilies:
Awake, O thou north-wind, and come thou
   South-wind, and blow on my garden
Till the spices flow out from the plants, that
   Bud in the light of His pardon.

At Rest.

O Power that can quicken from nought,
    Thou hast made my soul's barrenness fertile,
And the fir springs instead of the thorn, and
    Instead of the brier, the myrtle;
His hand holds me up lest I swerve
    From the path of His love and His meekness,
While I walk in the way He appoints, in
    The strength that is perfect in weakness.

Love and rest ! Rest and love ! Praise to God !
    And what if one worker have miss'd home,
Its comfort, its lovesome delight, for a
    Deep and a wonderful wisdom ?
Let him think how the Church may be served
    By his work, and rejoice without measure,
That Pain's furnace refined from the ore of
    Such work the good gold of His pleasure.

And if one, new-baptized in His grace, set the
    Seal of a grand consecration
On a life whose rath hours ran to waste,
    Who dareth doubt His acceptation?
The hour of love-work is worth twelve of
    Cold duty ; he serving most truly
Who loveth most deeply, and Christ the Rewarder
    Rewardeth each duly.

And well do we know that our God accepts the
    Least gift and the greatest,
Smiles down from His Majesty's height on
    The earliest workers and latest:

At Rest.

Gives strength to the faint, to the eyes that
  Up-yearn in their passionate duty,
The joy of the land far away where the
  King shall be seen in His beauty.

E. H. HICKEY.

THE DAILY COMMUNION.

BEFORE the dawn has streak'd the skies,
　　In the dim morning, cold and gray,
Thou sayest to my soul, "Arise,
　　Arise, my love, and come away."

* * * * *

Genesis xiv. 18.　Behold, the eternal King and Priest
　　Brings forth for thee the Bread and Wine;
Himself the Master of the Feast,
　　His very self the Food divine.

Should I not come when Thou dost call
　　Should I not eat at Thy command?
O Lord, my King, my Love, my All!
　　O wounded Heart, O piercèd Hand!

Why not? If sin and sorrow tire,
　　And make me yet unfit for Thee;
What is it, match'd with Thy "desire?"
　　"Do this in memory of Me."

Why not? Thou knowest all my heart,
　　My sins and stains to Thee are bare;
Cant. i. 7.　And since Thou tell'st me where Thou art,
　　There is my place, since Thou art there.

The Daily Communion.

Above all words is Thy command !
  Forgive, O Lord, each thought of sin ;
I bow myself beneath Thy Hand,
  O make me clean without; within !

So let me reach Thine altar, Lord,
  So humbly lift to Thee mine eyes ;
When veil'd upon the sacred Board,
  The pure, all-holy Offering lies.

* * * * *

I sleep—but let my heart still wake,
  Seeking for Thee throughout the night ;
Let holy dreams and musings make
  The hours of darkness warm and bright.

"Thou givest Thy beloved sleep :"   Psalm cxxvii. 3.
  Even in sleep my heart prepare,
And from all evil wanderings keep,   Cant. ii. 17.
  That none with Thee its love may share.

Thy hands have made and fashion'd me,   Psalm cxxxix. 4.
  Waking and sleep to Thee are one ;   and
And nothing is too hard for Thee   Psalm cxix. 73
  To finish that Thou hast begun.

By Thine own holy sleep, my Lord,
  Once dark and still on Mary's breast,
Or, with Thy fearful twelve on board,   S. Mark iv. 38.
  By wind and tempest sore distress'd,—

So ev'n in hours of weariness,
    When mind and tongue refuse to pray,
O do not love my soul the less,
    Nor take Thy precious care away!

Let my first waking thoughts be Thine;
    Awake me, Lord, to come to Thee;
Gleams, not of earth, around me shine;
    "I come, because Thou callest me."

Cant. vii. 12. 1st clause. How sweet for Thee to wake and rise
    Before the world begins her way;
To see Thy dawning in the skies
    Before the dawning of the day!

Cant. iv. 12. O! close mine eyes to all but Thee,
    Mine ears to every voice but Thine;
And let Thine Hand o'ershadow me
    While Thou art given to be mine!

Ah, what am I? and what art Thou?
    Ah, what am I that Thou shouldst come,
Stooping, to comfort me, so low—
    So wondrously to my poor home!

O! claim and bind this heart of mine
    That it may beat for Thee alone,
That it may lose its life in Thine,
    And have no will except Thine own.

Afflict and wound me, O my Lord,
    That I may sicken for Thy love,
Nor from that sickness be restored,
    Till laid before Thy Feet above.

The Daily Communion.

What freedom is there far from Thee?
　What joy if Thou from me art gone?
What comfort is there left for me
　Except in Thee, my Lord, alone?

O precious bonds, O blessèd pain!
　O dearly-loved captivity!
Strengthen each day, my Lord, the chain
　That binds me with sweet force to Thee.

Ah, what can harm if Thou art near?
　What do I need if Thou art mine?
I want no friend if Thou art here,
　Nor other's love if I have Thine!

In weariness be Thou my Rest,
　In loneliness be Thou my Friend;
In sorrow hold me to Thy breast,
　And make me love Thee to the end.

Be with me, Lord, through day and night,
　In every strife my soul sustain;
Till wakes me in the morning light
　The Voice of my Beloved again.　　*Cant. ii. 8.*

O! my "exceeding great Reward,"　　*Genesis xv. 1.*
　How sweet Thy latest call will be!
To be for "ever with the Lord,"
　Bound by eternal bonds to Thee!

J. R.

ON THE BIRTH OF VISCOUNT EDNAM, SON AND HEIR OF THE EARL OF DUDLEY.

RING out the bells from Dudley's ancient tower,
   Fill the glad air with song and festive lay;
Tell far the tidings of the priceless dower
   That thrills the Lord of Dudley's heart to-day.

Another link in the fair chain of love,
   Another brow the ancestral crown to wear;
God's precious gift of gladness from above,
   And of broad lands and fields a noble heir.

God bless the sleeping infant as he lies
   On the safe shelter of his mother's breast;
Guard his young years, and make him nobly wise
   With manly strength and gentle sweetness blest.

Unchanging like his motto: true and brave,
   A noble, earnest life to him be given;
Then, after the short slumber of the grave,
   A richer crown, as heir of highest Heaven.

R. H. BAYNES.

WESTWARD AND EASTWARD.

THEY look'd towards the West—
The Eden-exiles in their first amaze:
At the East Gate they saw the whirling blaze
That barr'd their way to rest.

The sun, to their dazed eyes,
Set black behind it: crush'd between, there lay,
Where God should no more walk at close of day,
An empty Paradise.

The hunger in their breast
Consumed them with the love of past delights;
And, yearning still through countless days and nights,
They look'd towards the West.

He look'd towards the West:
The statesman seer grown gray in Babylon
Long'd for the streets and walls his youth had known,
The towers he loved the best.

Stones of Jerusalem,
Ruins of a polluted sanctuary,
In his imperial captivity,
He turn'd toward them.

Westward and Eastward.

With empire sore opprest,
He laid down the world's weight at hours of prayer,
And seeking his heart's home, so far, so fair,
    He look'd towards the West.

We look towards the East:
Not to the garden,—all its flowers are dead;
Not to the city,—with Christ's life-blood red:
    All backward looks have ceased.

Ever we taste the Tree:
How poor and thin the Eden-life appears!
Peace without strife, joy without Christ-dried tears,
    Ignorant purity!

The City that we love
Is not a ruin, beauteous, incomplete,
Grow daily jasper wall and golden street,
    Jerusalem above!

The dawn is in the skies,
The morning of Creation's second birth;
And when the sun's first rays shall strike the earth
    The greeting song shall rise.

Therefore, at solemn Feast
And daily prayer, ere creed or praise begun,
We set our faces to the rising sun,
    And look towards the East.

                        M. A. M.

HOME!

(From the German of Karl Gerok.)

I WOULD go home,—home to my Father's dwelling,
    Home to my Father's breast;
    Far from the tempests that o'er earth are swelling,
    Into the deep, still rest.
The thousand hopes that once o'er life were cast,
Into one only longing hope have pass'd,
Now in my heart one aspiration springs,
    I would go home!

I would go home! I faint beneath thy sadness,
    O world where evil lies!
I would go home—I weary of the gladness
    That never satisfies.
Still will I bear my cross,—He wills it so,
Through the world's conflicts, still, His soldier, go.
Yet in my heart the murmur ever rings,
    I would go home!

I would go home, where, in some happy dreaming
    A better land I see,
I would be there, where endless light is streaming,
    Here is no rest for me.

Home.

The spring is past, the swallows rush through air,
O'er hill and vale, unstay'd by foe or snare,
O'er hill and vale they pass, on homeward wings :
    I would go home!

I would go home! the little child grows weary,
  And turns from feast or toy;
A little while, and all the mirth grows dreary,
  And he forgets his joy,
While yet his brother's eyes with glee are bright,
And laugh and pleasure scarce have reach'd their
    height,
Spite of earth's brightest fruits, earth's sweetest
    things :—
    I would go home!

I would go home,—the boat to port is pressing,
  The brook hastes to the sea,
The child is sleeping, hush'd in arms caressing,
  I, too, at rest would be.
Songs both of joy and sorrow I have heard;
Now, joy is silent, grief a vacant word,
One song alone, the last my spirit sings,—
    I would go home!

                      AUGUSTA C. HAYWARD.

AN EVENING PRAYER.

Y Father! God of life and light,
    Ere evening's hour hath ebb'd away,
Before Thy throne of grace to-night
    I offer up this closing day.

Fresh from Thy hand, this morn it rose
    Divinely fair, sublimely meet;
I bring it back at evening's close,—
    Alas! how changed, how incomplete!

One plea alone my heart can claim
    For such a tribute, soil'd and dim,—
I offer it in Jesu's Name,
    Make Thou its darkness light in Him.

I bring Thee all this day hath brought,
    Its storm and sunshine, joy and pain;
Its every word and deed and thought;
    Its hope and fear, its loss and gain.

I bring to Thee, to purify
    Its few faint thoughts of Thee and Heaven;
I bring Thee all its tears to dry,
    And all its sins to be forgiven.

I lay before Thy pitying gaze
    Its joys to bless, its wounds to cure;
I bring it all to speak Thy praise,
    And tell of Thy compassion sure.

An Evening Prayer.

And now, O Lord my God, or ere
  This day in sleep forgotten be,
Its dying breath must rise in pray'r
  And bear my latest thought to Thee.

And since, perchance, no morrow's light
  May greet mine ear with wakening call,
In Thy good care I leave this night
  Myself, my life, my heart, mine all.

The loved ones, those I hold so dear,
  Be pleased, sweet Lord, to guard and keep,
To all their hearts this night draw near,
  And tend and bless them while they sleep.

My human love, so incomplete,
  Where can its longings find their rest,
Except to lay them at Thy feet,
  Who knowest all, and lovest best?

On eyes that weep, on hearts that bleed,
  May all Thy richest blessings fall;
I ask Thy help for all who need,
  And asking this, I pray for all.

And if to morn in safety brought,
  Grant that sweet breathings, pure and true,
May rest on each awakening thought,
  As on fresh flowers the early dew.

Thus, Lord, this night I yield to Thee;
  Or if I sleep, or if I wake,
Whate'er I have, whate'er I be,
  Bid me good night for Jesu's sake.

M. L. B.

GOOD FRIDAY.

 HANDS outstretch'd for me,
Upon the bitter 'Tree
Through all those weary hours of mortal
pain,
Loosen the iron bands
That chain my captive hands,
And set me free to serve my God again.

"O wounded Feet, for me
Nail'd to the accursèd Tree,
Walk still before me in life's narrow way;
Guide to heaven's pasture sweet
My wayworn, wandering feet
In the right path, O never more to stray.

"O sacred Heart, for me
Pierced on that saddest Tree,
Ne'er through life's years may thy deep pity cease;
Guide Thou my changeful heart,
Guide it to where Thou art,
Blest with Thy blessing, compass'd with Thy peace."

REV. HERBERT TODD.

DEATH IN THE FOLD.

 LAMB is dead!
    And there is bitter wailing in the fold ·
For that sweet lamb upon its bed
    Which lieth senseless, lifeless, cold,
Was one so pure, so soft, so mild,
So very stainless and undefiled,
  It had just begun to skip and play
In joyous glee by its mother's side,
  When sickness seiz'd it, and it pined away
Until it died!

Lament no more!
  Seeing it died the sacred fold within;
It had enter'd through that only door
  Where all must pass who life would win;
And on its forehead fair there shone
The mark of the Shepherd's sheep alone.
  Therefore His lamb that Shepherd drew
From out the desert land of wrath;
  And by that mark its present safety knew,
And watch'd its path!

Couldst thou have been
  Where the angels were, and as the angels know,
Surely thou a sight hadst seen
  To dry thy tears ere they might flow,

Beside its couch, the Man who gave
His very life that lamb to save :
   Thou wouldst have seen thy darling laid
Sooth'd and pillow'd on His breast,
   Till by one brightest spirit thence convey'd,
At peace, at rest !

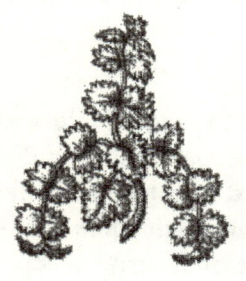

"REPROBATE SILVER."

(*Jer.* vi. 30.)

"WE have eaten in Thy presence; Thou hast taught within our streets."
Glorious in His beauty shining from the everlasting seats!
Hark! upon the shores of gladness how the billowy music beats!

Faintly, vaguely, downward floating comes a sweet celestial chime,
Earnest of a glorious future, mindful of a happy prime,
Drowning in oblivious silence all the shadowy songs of time.

Nearer now, and ever fairer, rise to view the golden towers!
Clearer still, and ever sweeter flows the music from the bowers!
Lo! the world, and life, and all things to eternity are ours!

Brothers, joy! before us lying see the shining prize we sought!
Not unmindful is the Master of the works that we have wrought,
In His name who cast out devils—in His mighty name Who taught.

Lord, O Lord! Thy servants wait Thee—wait their
    Master's smile to win!
Lord, O Lord! Thy saints implore Thee, sanctified
    from earth and sin,
Let the children of the kingdom to their heritage
    come in.

Then, as through the gold of sunset gleams a solitary
    star,
Flash'd a light above all other, and for answer, clear
    and far,
Came a voice which said, "Depart ye, for I know
    not whence ye are!"

CHARLES LAWRENCE FORD, B.A.

ST. MICHAEL'S VICTORY.

GUIDO'S PICTURE OF "THE TRIUMPH OF ST. MICHAEL OVER SATAN," IN THE CHURCH OF THE CAPUCHINS, ROME.

"But is it thus that Virtue looks, the moment after its death-struggle with evil?"—N. HAWTHORNE, *Transformation*.

MICHAEL, bright Archangel, calmly standing
In holy triumph o'er thy master'd foe;
Thine eyes are tranquil, and thy front commanding,
While Satan, foil'd and vanquish'd, shrinks below.

And not a feather of thy silvery pinion
   Is ruffled by the struggle; not a trace
Of all it cost thee to obtain dominion
   Is visible on thine exalted face.

Thy radiant sword is in thine hand unbroken,
   No stain upon thy vesture may be seen;
Nor is there here portray'd the faintest token
   To show the mighty conflict that hath been!

Was it so quickly won, that "war in heaven?"
   And was the great "Accuser" put to flight
With scarce an effort? and the victory given
   So easily to thee, Archangel bright?

St. Michael's Victory.

Not so; the strife was terrible: around thee
   Thy bright battalions rallied; thou didst wage
No light-won battle, though the Dragon found thee
   Too strong for his dark legions' gather'd rage.

Far truer had the painter's pencil shown thee
   With garments rent, locks wild, and white plumes
      torn;
Then as the victor every eye should own thee,
   By all these signs of bitter conflict borne.

Dost thou look down on us when dread temptations
   Threaten to drag us to the depths of sin,
And all the hosts of evil inclinations
   Assist the force without by foes within?

And dost thou see us weeping, struggling, fighting,
   Until our feeble powers are well-nigh spent?
Now beaten to the dust, now fiercely smiting
   Those evil "messengers" our foe hath sent.

Pierced with red wounds that leave the heart-blood
      flowing,
   Weary with lifting up the cross and sword;
Faint with the conflict long-sustain'd, yet knowing
   That with us are the angels of the Lord!

Oh, "more than conquerors" at last! but bearing
   The marks of every battle that we fought;
Leaving the field triumphant, yet still wearing
   Those scars which tell the day was dearly bought.

And thoughtful eyes may read the outward traces
  Of silent struggle, in the graver mien,
And furrows deeply graven on some faces,
  Where once no lines of care were ever seen.

Oh, bright Archangel, not by our poor merit,
  But by the power that won the strife for thee,
We conquer, till God calls us to inherit
  The spoils of war—the crowns of victory!

HARTLEBURY CASTLE,

The Seat of the Lord Bishop of Worcester,
July, MDCCCLXX.

SURE on no fairer, sweeter spot than this,
    The golden beams of early sunlight fall;
    The summer breezes straying, love to kiss
    The leaves that cluster round the chapel-wall.

Below—the calm still lake that seems to bring
    A sense of coolness e'en in sultriest hours;
And round its border stately trees that fling
    Their welcome shadow on the grass and flowers.

Around—the fruitful fields and song of bird,
    Glimpses of cedars, rows of fragrant limes;
The dream-like stillness only faintly stirr'd
    By the sweet music of the village chimes.

Within—an English home, where truth and love
    And gentlest courtesies all sweetly blend;
Faint image of that brighter home above,
    Towards which our faltering steps should ever tend.

Here, 'mid the heat and burden of the day,
    Dear memories of its gladness linger yet;
The quiet chapel where we knelt to pray,
    The earnest voice that none will e'er forget.

Peace to this house ! and all who in it dwell,
  And God's rich benediction ; and the joy
Of His dear Presence—joy no words may tell,
  That earth can never give, nor e'er destroy.

His firm yet gentle rule long may he bear,
  Who, like the Master, doth not drive, but leads
The flock of Christ, and with unwearied care,
  That flock redeem'd, with wholesome doctrine feeds.

Then, his work over, and the victory won—
  The burden of the flesh laid meekly down—
Christ greet him with His blessed words, "Well done,"
  And for earth's mitre give heaven's glorious crown !

R. H. Baynes.

"THE FAITHFUL IN THE LORD'S SUPPER."

KEEP we the Feast, with solemn joy, too holy
    For souls untuned as yet to love divine,
    While all deep rapture fills the hearts low-bending,
      Where the incarnate God
      Bestows His flesh and blood
On His own faithful ones, beneath the sign
Of broken Bread, and of outpourèd Wine.
Keep we the Feast of Feasts to-day, for Christ,
Our Passover, for us is sacrificed.

O virgin-spirits, robed in blood-wash'd raiment,
  Ye through all veils of clay discern the grace,
The glory of the King, Who bids you banquet
      On Food more pure and sweet
      Than what the Angels eat.
Immanuel—God with us—how the place
Flames with the splendour of His lovely Face.
Keep we the Feast of Feasts to-day, for Christ,
Our Passover, for us is sacrificed.

88 "*The Faithful in the Lord's Supper.*"

Here, dearest Lord, this all transcendent glory,
   Thou shed'st alone on those whose wills are bent
To Thine in fearless love and reverent meekness;
      Whose being utterly
      Yearns ever up to Thee;
Whose ev'ry thought, hope, joy, with Thee is blent,
Who live Thy Life of Love, in Sacrament
Receive Thee, feed on Thee: for these, Thou Christ,
Our Passover, indeed art sacrificed.

O come the day when the unsinning spirit
   No more shall sob and shiver 'neath the stress
Of this mysterious mingled joy and sorrow,
      But in the perfect Rest
      Of God made manifest,
Feast, hour by hour, upon the loveliness
Of the fair Face, once marr'd for our distress,
Needing no more, or Sacrament or sign,
Lord, Thou for ever ours, and we for ever Thine.

SIT ANIMA MEA CUM EJUS ANIMA!

THOU hast cross'd the troubled waters,
    Thou hast reach'd the happy shore,
Thou hast striven with temptation,
    Thou wilt strive no more.
      O, I envy thee!

We are toiling still in rowing,
    Winds are raging, waves run high;
Faith and courage often failing;
    No deliverer nigh.
      O, I envy thee!

Shall I e'er again be with thee?
    Shall I ever win the rest,
Where thy happy soul reposeth
    On that loving Breast?
      O, I envy thee!

Sometimes I have had a vision
    Of the clear, calm, crystal sea—
Caught a prospect of the haven
    Where my soul would be,
      Dearest, safe with thee.

Sit Anima mea cum ejus Anima!

Sometimes o'er the troubled waters
  I have thought I heard thy voice,
Calling, " Cheer thee, brother, cheer thee
  Thou shalt yet rejoice,
    Yes, rejoice with me !"

But again the dark clouds gather,
  And again the billows roll,
Shutting out the distant prospect,
  Shutting in my soul.
    O, I envy thee !

Ah ! another voice is calling
  High above the tempest's roar ;
And a glorious Form is standing
  On the distant shore :—
    Doth He call to me ?

Yes, my soul, to thee He calleth ;
  Thou shouldst know those accents blest—
" He that to the end endureth
  Wins the promised rest."
    Lord, I wait for Thee !

            F. W. HARRIS, M. A.

HARVEST HYMN.

WE praise Thee, God our Father,
   For love unask'd, untold;
We bless Thee, God the Giver,
   For mercies manifold.
We sing the special bounty
   Which prospers us once more,
And fills again so richly
   Our basket and our store.

For who but Thou, most Mighty,
   Could give each seed its birth,
And place the crown of plenty
   Upon the smiling earth?
Or who could give when needed
   The late and early rain,
Or send the blessed sunbeams
   To swell the golden grain?

If on the sinless only
   Thy ceaseless gifts should fall,
Which of us, Lord, should merit
   The smallest boon of all?
Ah, no! Thou hast not meted
   Thy goodness by our worth;
Heaven's bounty is not fetter'd
   By all the guilt of earth.

Harvest Hymn.

O help us, Lord, to labour
  For that eternal Bread,—
The Meat that cannot perish,
  Whereby our souls are fed;
And lead us on and upward,
  When we would wayward roam,
That we may share the glory
  Of Thine own Harvest Home.

E. P.

"BLESSED ARE THE PURE IN HEART: FOR THEY SHALL SEE GOD."

OF all the lovely seven
    Beatitudes that Heaven
To the true saints of Jesus doth impart,
    Is any one more sweet
    Than that which bends to greet
The yearning vision of the pure in heart?

    With joy the Father shall
    Welcome the prodigal,
Go forth with Love's wide arms His child to meet;
    And bid His servants bring
    For him the hallow'd ring,
And the best robe, and sandals for his feet.

    Yet oh! more deeply blest,
    About whose holy breast
The chrism's candent folds all stainless shine,—
    First in his Father's heart,
    Sayeth He, "Son, thou art
Ever with Me, and all I have is thine."

    Seal'd with Thy grace unpriced,
    Thy life in him, O Christ!
Thy Body and Thy Blood in mystery sweet

"Blessed are the Pure in Heart:

      His hunger ever feed,
      And quench his thirst indeed,
Till to Thy home Thou bring his pilgrim feet.

      Him with thy Spirit graced
      Thou sufferedst not to taste
Of the world's broken cisterns, hewn to mock
      The thirst, but mad'st him know
      The draughts of life that flow
From Thy cleft Heart, O deeply smitten Rock.

      Thou draw'st Him, Spotless One !
      So doth he swiftly run
In those dear-blood mark'd footprints after Thee ;
      With all of life inwrought
      Art Thou, and every thought
Brought into Thy divine captivity.

      Thou sett'st him on the height
      Of mountains of delight,
With rapturous odours surging round his feet ;
      While deep his ravished brain
      Drinks the ecstatic strain
Of bird-shrined seraphim, supremely sweet.

      Oh bliss beyond all dreams—
      Through rifted skies there streams
The dawn of that great glory that shall be,
      And wraps and folds him round
      And all is hallowed ground
Where he, the pure in heart, his God doth see.

And all with God doth blend,
Even when he must descend—
O God! all sweetness doubly sweet in Thee!
Each smile and tear shall prove
The diverse forms of love—
Each common meal a very Agape.

The sacrifice of Christ
In him is realized—
Life—Christ—he knows the holy synonym;
And treading where He trod
He sees his Saviour-God
Where souls less white can but feel after Him.

He, whose earth's glory is,
Reads type of the deep bliss
Of splendid beauty in the Father's home;
The while another's gaze
Sees in the scarlet blaze
Only the mystic Harlot's cursed chrome.

For, breathing clearer air
Than grosser souls can bear,
Of hills he clomb unsobbing, undistress'd,
He bathes his eagle sight
In the all-perfect light
Of His bright Face, who is The Loveliest.

His fervid charity
As golden bands must be
For the lost found, lest any more he rove;

"Blessed are the Pure in Heart;

      Holding in holy bliss
      This fellowship of his
With the All-pure, All-Strong, whose name is Love.

      Where passion's storms uncheck'd
      The Baptism-hope have wrecked,
And the Cross-banner smirched and torn may be,
      His help outstretch'd will prove
      In grand, unshrinking love,
Even here the pure in heart his God doth see.

      Yet in deep self-distrust
      He counts himself unjust,
Unholy, in His eyes, by Whom is prized,
      Above all offerings,
      The lowly heart that clings
To the dear Cross that took the life of Christ.

      Blest through this little while
      That faith through tears must smile,
And patience keep her stately sweet control;
      Love's eager feet a space
      Be hindered in the race,
And but in part the knowledge of the soul:

      Till He, the Strong and True,
      Who maketh all things new,
In His best, wisest season, set the child
      Who is beloved of Him
      Beyond His cherubim,
In the dear kingdom of the undefiled.

Oh fellowship divine,
For which we want and pine!
Oh blessedness beyond the angels' ken!
Oh prayer, whose strength and sum
Is, Come, thou Bridegroom, come;
Even so, come quickly, JESUS CHRIST. AMEN.

E. H. HICKEY.

"THAT THEY ALL MAY BE ONE."

AND doth Thy last deep longing yet remain,
    All through long ages still a thing undone?
Hath prayer of Thine gone up to Heaven in vain,
    O Thou Eternal Son?

Thy heart's desire, can it then be of nought?
    An aimless wish; to be remembered not,
Nor leave a trace? Hath She, so dearly bought,
    That deep desire forgot?

Hath God not heard it? Doth He hear the cry
    Of the young ravens asking Him for food,
Yet pass the prayer of His Beloved One by,
    For all His tears and blood?

Was it for this that precious stream outwelled
    Upon the thirsty desert of the earth;
That Thy last legacy should thus be held
    Light and of little worth?

Thy legacy of Peace is spent and gone!
    Thy vesture torn and scattered far and wide;
A scorn and stumbling-block! True hearts make moan.
    Thine enemies deride.

"That they All may be One."

"That they may all be one, as Thou in Me,
   And I in Thee, O Father!" Shall that cry
Of Thy deep heart a thing forgotten be,
      And so forgotten, die?

Nay; then, forbid it, Lord! Lo, now Thy Spouse
   Seeks Thee in humbleness and deep desire!
Renew in her the joy of her first vows,
      The Pentecostal Fire

That drew all hearts in one: O Love! O Light!
   Shine forth, to purge, to quicken, to restore,
Till She again be beauteous in Thy sight,
      And knit in love once more!

Ay, chasten if Thou wilt! So all untruth
   And all un-love die off and drop away;
Till purified by fire as in Her youth,
      Her light shine forth as day.

Till growing ever closer to their Head,
   Her long estranged ones draw more near each other,
Into all Truth by One blest Spirit led,
      As children of one Mother.

"One Flock, one Shepherd;" this, Thy promise, Lord!
   Teach Her to pray for it in ceaseless strain;
Teach her to plead Thine own, Thy plighted word,
      Nor plead with Thee in vain.

Teach Her for this to strive, to hope, to yearn;
  For this no toil, no sacrifice to shun,
Till all dear ties of sisterhood return,
      And all are Thine, and One!

E. H.

POEMS FROM THE BIBLE.

"His own City."—*Matt.* ix. 1.

THRONED on a sea of gold, upheaves a
    cluster of columns—
    Steals through the arch of Time the long
    lost music of Eden—
Here, through yon shattered porch, the gossamer
    step of some maiden
Fell to the music's fall, as falls a fairy-like snowflake
On the green holly-sheen, in wreath of virginal
    whiteness!

Over these craggy slopes, oft roamed His lingering
    footsteps,
Straying beside this lake, where softly, ripple on
    ripple,
Dreamily plashed on His ear, the mystic song of the
    waters.

What were the "mighty works" He did in the
    might of His manhood?
Tell me, ye sullen cliffs, thou mocking mirror of
    heaven,
Have ye no trace of His life, no grand old-world
    recollections?

Is this another loss? and must oblivion sweep
    onward,
Blotting His feet from the sand beneath the murmuring surges?
In the dim straggling light, must doubt glide on like
    a spectre,
Whispering that god-like words oft end in terrible
    failure?

Rose-gleams over the lake, sinks down my soul as I
    wander,
Looking for long-lost graves, 'mid dreams of fluttering
    footsteps,—
Lattices filled at eve with peals of silvery laughter,—
White arms kissed by the moon, while every breeze
    from the hill-side
Sped with the breath of flowers, Nature's tremulous
    love-song!

Here, in this narrow street, was this the linen-veil'd
    doorway,
Where every wanderer stayed on his lip the song he
    was singing,
And thinking of Him who lived there, paused soft
    to murmur a blessing—

Lived here the Virgin mother, and he, the beloved
    disciple:
Or was He lone in His life, and rising in the red
    morning,

Paced He these starlit downs, while His own city
    was sleeping—
Kept He His vigils for God, the Lord of terrible
    future?

Say shall His city see Him, when with the trump of
    the Judgment
He lights on Sion again, and calls His slumbering
    children?
Will He come back to these heaps, and save from
    desolate ruin
Memories of youth and home, the ghastly story of
    failure
That shadowed His work on earth? will He publish
    anew His love-poem?

In the great world of light, will He make His Life as
    the noon-day?
Shall the unwritten be clear, and for His children
    who waited,
Christ be the moonlit path o'er the dread abysses of
    knowledge?

ALAN BRODRICK, B.A.

"COMFORT YE."

YE whose hearts with grief and sin are dreary,
    Wandering footsore on this barren sod,
Hear this voice, which speaketh to the
    weary,
'Comfort ye My people,' saith your God.

"I your Shepherd, vigilant and tender,
    Feed My flock, and gather with My arm—
All who labour with their hearts to render
    Love and trust, I keep them safe from harm

"Weep no more, Jerusalem's sad daughters,
    Weary, heaven-laden, come to Me;
All that thirst, O come unto the waters,
    'Comfort ye My people, comfort ye.'

"Though the Evil one, with vile temptations
    Striveth through your minds your soul to win;
If ye spurn his base insinuations,
    I will keep your spirit safe within.

"Fear not, though the mists of sense assail you,
    I will bring you to the perfect day,
My great mercy richly shall avail you,
    Send My messenger to smoothe the way.

" Though the cruel doubts which oft distress you,
  Bring your feeble gifts of thanks and praise;
Freely then the light of faith shall bless you,
  Mountains lowering, lowly valleys raise.

" Crooked paths shall straight become before you,
  While o'er rugged ways ye smoothly go.
Now ye know not how My arm is o'er you,
  But hereafter ye shall surely know.

" To pure snow, your sins of scarlet turning,
  Crimson-dyed, they white as wool shall be;
My refining fire in you is burning:
  If I wash you, ye have part in Me."

Christ! dear Christ! as Heaven than earth is higher,
  Is Thy mercy greater than our sin;
Walk with us unharmed amid the fire,
  Carry Thy weak lambs Thy fold within.

E. MOULTRIE.

EVENING HYMN.

HERE do I wait to greet
 The sound of Thy dear feet,
 With eyes uplifted in the dewy calm;
 Now the day-burden's stress
 Hath ceased to strain and press,
And sweetly solemn sounds the vesper psalm.

 Come, for I pant to know
 The love that draws me so,
Drowns earth in heaven, earth's will drowns in
  heaven's will:
 Come and abide with me,
 For Thou alone art He
Who can My spirit's thirst and hunger fill.

 Long ago didst Thou say,
 " Arise and come away,
Thy winter-time of doubts and fears is past."
 Then did I gird my brow
 With splendour of my vow,
And clung about Thy feet and held Thee fast.

 What in the Shulamite
 Can move Thee with delight,

Evening Hymn.

What loveliness, O Thou most lovely one?
    What beauty canst Thou trace
    In her uplifted face,
Dark from the noontide glare of the strong sun?

    Yet dost Thou bid her prove
    Immeasurable love;
So now she lies at peace upon Thy breast,
    With all her moanings still'd,
    And every yearning fill'd
With the strong joy of Thine exceeding rest.

WATCHING.

"When the Son of Man cometh, shall He find faith on the earth?"
S. Luke xviii. 8.

WHEN Thy virgins' lamps are burning,
   While the slow hours creep,
Wilt Thou suddenly returning
   Break their weary sleep?

When the busy hands are idle
   And the strong hearts fail,
Will the summons to the Bridal
   Rend the cloudy veil?

When the crimson morning faintly
   O'er the East shall break,
Will there be no spirits saintly
   Watching for Thy sake?

Will there be no faithful servant
   Looking for Thy sign?
Prayerful, hopeful, strong and fervent,
   Fill'd with love divine;

Love, that ever more remembers
   All the old desires,
Fanning still the glowing embers
   Of its beacon fires!

Watching.

Yea, upon the wind-swept heather
    Of the cloudy hill,
Christian souls keep watch together,
    Waiting for Thee still.

Yea, within the valleys lowly,
    On the quiet sod,
Christian hearts keep vigil holy
    For the Son of God.

In the great world's crowded places
    Some whose hopes are high,
Listen with uplifted faces
    For the Herald's cry:

Trusting, pleading, weeping, fearing,
    Scorning earthly things;
Through the wild sin-revel hearing
    Sounds of angel-wings.

Sorrowful, yet fill'd with gladness,
    Bound,—yet always free;
Strangers in a land of sadness,—
    Yet well known to Thee.

Poor,—yet often richly giving
    From their secret hoard;
Dying daily,—and yet living
    Ever to the Lord.

These are Thine;—O Bridegroom, hear them
    When their cries ascend!
Let Thy Comforter be near them
    Till their watch shall end.

Guard them,—till Thine angel loudly
  Sounds the trumpet blast,
And Thou comest, crownèd proudly,
  As a King, at last !

SARAH DOUDNEY.

HOME-SICKNESS.

"I AM the resurrection, and the life:"
 O comfort one another with these
  words,
 When the sad heart, o'erwearied with the
  strife,
Lies as the wither'd leaves and broken sherds.

When the bright thought of what one hand might
  dare
 Is cross'd by darker thought of years half done,
And Hope, false guide, that spoke at morn so fair,
 Shows us at night our journey but begun;

When loving hearts, their early freshness lost,
 As flowers that feel no more the morning dew,
Look back, amid the sereness and the frost,
 With wonder on the spring-time that they knew;

When that one fault from which we deem'd secure
 Our guarded heart at last too well discern'd
Leaves us, while less of our own goodness sure,
 O'erwhelm'd with shame that we so late have
  learn'd;

When, eager with intenseness of desire,
   Some evil path to flee, some grace to win,
Our will consenting not, some cross of·fire
   Drives us, perforce, to weakness or to sin;

When prayer of faith for needful seeming things
   Returns unanswer'd, as some cry for rain
Is heeded not, till in its season flings
   The cloud unask'd its fulness on the plain;

When every simple, unpresumptuous scheme
   Our humble path in quiet peace to take
Is broken like a bubble or a dream,
   And every morning to fresh care we wake;

When loving trust by selfish craft is wiled,
   And they who fear not God are prosper'd most,
And he who walks with pureness of a child
   Loses his right, while they who wrong'd him boast;

When what we fear'd, but bravely strove to shun,
   Seems for the shunning all the while more near,
As some black cloud that will not be outrun
   O'ertakes and rolls its thunder in our ear;

When the soul's cheerful smile, like summer blue,
   Is clouded by the body's mystic laws,
And life, defrauded of her rightful due,
   Lies helpless as a bird in eagle's claws:—

Home-Sickness.

Oh, then, as comes to Switzer far exiled
    The "Ranz des Vaches" amid the Moslem
        palms,
Ringing him back his Alpine forest wild,
    Glacier, and herd, and sweet Waldensian psalms,

Till his eyes close, and all his heart is far,
    Far from the perilous fight or footsore march,—
Far in the chalet, where the morning star
    Shines cold and clear on the snow-laden larch;

So on our ears shall fall this heavenly strain,
    Singing of home with all sweet memories rife.
O Saviour! sound it in our hearts again!
    Be now the Resurrection and the Life!

                CHARLES LAWRENCE FORD, B.A.

CHRISTMAS.

OVER moor and over mere,
    Sentinell'd by watching stars,
Ring the chimes out sharp and clear.
    Listening over Heaven's bars
Angels hear the song again,
    Sung by angels years ago,
Over Bethlehem's silent plain,
    When dark Earth was white with snow.

Over mere and over moor,
    Still with the fast-falling flake,
Rising up to Heaven's floor,
    Spreading over swamp and brake,
Up and down ring forth the chimes,
    For the World, or old or young,
For both late and early times,—
    All for whom the angels sung.

Over mountain, dell, and wold,
    Hush'd of moil and sin the strife,
Strange the silence as of old
    When broke songs divine of life.
From our heavenward-pointing spires,
    Up to yonder star-sprent sky,
Trembling chimes and earthly choirs—
    Glory be to God on high.

Christmas.

While from out the open door
   Gleams flash forth across the snow,
Where within, on marble floor,
   Crowd adoring hearts below:
Starry lights in clusters hung,
   Echoes of first Christmas morn,
Rising, falling tones outsung—
   Unto us a Child is born.

Old the love of God for man,
   New the grace shed over all,
Marvellous His mighty plan
   To reverse our parents' fall.
Mary's joys all fresh for aye,
   Ever welcome Christmas time,
Blessed song for gladsome day—
   Glorious burden on the chime.

Chime o'er moor, then, and o'er mere,
   Chime for old and chime for young,
Never heed the dying Year
   So our Christmas song be sung:
Praise and worship, as we sing
   Of a grace-replenish'd store,
Jesus, Child, Redeemer, King,
   Who brought Peace for evermore.

FREDERICK GEORGE LEE.

HIS COMING.

AGAIN, O Lord! Thy Church the song
    is swelling
    That hails Thine advent to Thine
    earthly home!
Again her priests the tale of Him are telling,
  Who suddenly did to His Temple come.

Again they tell us of the eternal glory,
  That when He comes again, shall in Him be;
And bid us, pondering on His mortal story,
  Wait till His second advent dread we see.

Another hour of earthly night has fleeted,
  Yet from the promised morning beams no ray;
An hour of care and grief again repeated,
  And yet we see not the eternal day.

And heavier is the load that we are bearing,
    And darker shades of sin have veil'd our sight,
More solemn and more sad the night is wearing,
    More distant seems the daybreak's glimmering
    light.

But we can hear Thee the glad word pronouncing,—
  "The daylight is at hand"—and fear no more;
The works of darkness in Thy trust renouncing,
  Armour of light around us evermore.

So we press forward, never backward turning
  Our lingering looks to where, in western skies,
Earth's setting hopes with a dim light are burning,
  But eastward gazing, where the day shall rise.

Till o'er the everlasting hills the dawning
  Shall break at length in fulness, till we see,
Amid the light of the eternal morning,
  Thy second advent's glorious majesty.

A. C. HAYWARD.

THE YEARS THAT ARE GONE.

LOST are the years gone by? We hold
    them still,
  While over their course of light or dark-
    ness brooding,
We clasp them and they fly not, ne'er eluding
  The effort of the memory's love-strong will.

Voices we hear we deem'd for ever dumb;
Catches on memory's ear the sudden thrilling;
Starting, we look if earth again be filling
  With beings gone, no more again to come.

Into life's solitude our burden bearing,
Tears falling when alone we seem to wander,—
Fell not unseen; for mystic figures yonder
  Move o'er the space, a human likeness wearing.

Those forms, ofttimes invisible, we see
Through the thick mists around us darkly spreading
Across the boundary of existence, treading
  Into the solemn light of memory.

In human shape they come, yet not entire
The mortal mould: on their reposing features
Burns not the brand impress'd on mortal creatures
  Of iron, heated in affliction's fire.

Theirs is the peace, by life's rude shocks unbroken;
Theirs the white robes seen but in shadowy dreaming;
Theirs the unearthly glory strangely gleaming,
  Of their new world the bright unfading token.

Yes, ours the vanish'd years—they cannot die;
Held with a loving bond in our hearts' keeping,
They are not dead; oft from their peaceful sleeping,
  Waking to bid us, where they beckon, fly.

A. C. HAYWARD.

IN MEMORY OF BISHOP PATTESON.

HATH He who reaps the wheat and leaves
  the tares,
Who saves the rotten tree and fells the
  sound,
No hidden purpose in the will that spares
  The cumberers of the ground?

Thousands will live their lives, unloved, unblest;
Long selfish lives of sinful sloth and ease,
While he—the Martyr Bishop—lies at rest
  In the far Southern Seas.

Better like him to spend a busy day,
Than pass whole years in idle waste and wrong,
For truly saith the poet in his lay
  That "no true life is long."

Better to die for love of God and man,
Than live for lower aims and baser deeds,
Better to die "in faith"—than live to scan
  Flaws in our neighbours' creeds.

He needs no praise of human lip or pen,
Nor "storied window" in the minster high,
His name is graven in the hearts of men,
  His works will never die.

In Memory of Bishop Patteson.

Soon shall the precious seed his hands have sown,
A goodly growth of golden blessings yield;
A fairer monument than carven stone
    Is that rich harvest field.

So let us leave him—is it not in vain
On God's decrees to spend our idle breath?
Enough for us to live—and humbly gain
    Strength from the Martyr's death.

SARAH DOUDNEY.

NOTHING BUT LEAVES.

AVIOUR, comest Thou to me
Seeking fruit upon Thy tree?
Shall I render naught to Thee?

Lively faith and holy deeds
Springing from His precious seeds,
Are the fruit the Searcher needs.

Shall His love and tender care,
Gifts of light and dew and air,
Win no guerdon for Him there?

Oft the Holy Spirit grieves
O'er the promise that deceives,
Seeking fruit, He finds but leaves:

Fair pretence and pleasant show
Hiding barrenness below,
Vain profession, working woe.

Only leaves ;—O patient Lord,
After all Thy tears outpour'd
Shalt Thou find such poor reward?

After all Thy toil and pain,
Some return for love to gain,
Master, shalt Thou seek in vain?

Nothing but Leaves.

Lest I prove a worthless tree,
Send Thy plenteous grace to me;
Let me bring forth fruit to Thee.

SARAH DOUDNEY.

BOAZ ASLEEP.

(Translated from the French of Victor Hugo.)

T work within his barn since very early,
   Fairly tired out with toiling all the day,
   Upon the small bed where he always
      lay,
Boaz was sleeping by his sacks of barley.

Barley and wheat fields he possess'd, and well,
   Though rich, loved justice; wherefore all the flood
   That turn'd his mill wheels was unstain'd with
      mud,
And in his smithy blazed no fire of hell.

His beard was silver, as in April all
   A stream may be. He did not grudge a stook;
   When the poor gleaners pass'd, with kindly look,
Quoth he, "Of purpose let some handfuls fall."

He walk'd his way of life straight on and plain,
   With justice clothed, like linen white and clean;
   And ever rustling towards the poor, I ween,
Like public fountains ran his sacks of grain.

Good master, faithful friend, in his estate
   Frugal yet generous, beyond the youth
   He won regard of woman, for in sooth
The young man may be fair—the old man's great.

Boaz Asleep.

Life's primal source, unchangeable and bright,
    The old man entereth, the day eterne;
    And in the young man's eye a flame may burn,
But in the old man's eye one seeth light.

As Jacob slept, or Judith, so full deep
    Slept Boaz 'neath the leaves. Now it betided,
    Heaven's gate being partly open, that there glided
A fair dream forth, and hover'd o'er his sleep.

And in his dream to heaven, the blue and broad,
    Right from his loins an oak tree grew amain,
    His race ran up it far, like a long chain!
Below it sang a king, above it died a God.

Whereupon Boaz murmur'd in his heart,
    The number of my years is past four score.
    How may this be? I have not any more
A son, or wife; yea she who had her part

In this my couch, O Lord! is now in Thine;
    And she half living, I half dead within,
    Our beings still commingle and are twin;
It cannot be that I should found a line!

" Youth hath triumphant mornings; its days bound
    From night as from a victory. But such
    A trembling as the birch tree's to the touch
Of winter is on all, and evening closes round.

" I bow my soul to death, as kine to meet
    The water bow their fronts athirst." He said,
    The cedar feeleth not the rose's head,
Nor he the woman's presence at his feet!

For while he slept, the Moabitess Ruth
    Lay at his feet, expectant of his waking,
    He knowing not what sweet guile she was making,
She knowing not what God would have in sooth.

Asphodel scents did Gilgal's breezes bring ;—
    Through nuptial shadows, questionless, full fast
    The angels sped, for momently there pass'd
A something blue which seem'd to be a wing.

Silent was all in Jezreel and Ur—
    The stars were glittering in the heaven's dark meadows ;
    Far west among those flowers of the shadows,
The thin clear crescent, lustrous over her,

Made Ruth raise question, looking through the bars
    Of heaven, with eyes half-oped, what God, what comer
    Unto the harvest of the eternal summer,
Had flung his golden hook down on the field of stars.

        W. ALEXANDER, D.D., *Bishop of Derry
        and Raphoe.*

CHRIST AND THE LITTLE CHILD.

PERCHANCE it is an idle thought,
   Yet fancy unreproved may deem,
That not alone for lessons taught,
   Pride-humbling, scorning man's esteem,
Visions of worldly hope to dim,
He call'd the little child to Him.

But watching him at harmless play,
   With all unutterable love,
He drew him with that glance away
   Which charms the seraphim above;
And tender was the grasp that press'd
That loving infant to His breast.

And sweet was the repose He found
   In childish nature, simple, free;
While all around, with jarring sound,
   Rose the loud strife for mastery,
From worldly hearts, as yet untaught,
Of heavenly crown by suffering bought.

O Saviour! when our selfish pride
   Would cause Thy Spirit to depart,
Be our affections mortified!
   Give us the little children's heart!
Allure us by Thy mightier will,
And put thine arms about us still.

            CHARLES LAWRENCE FORD, B.A.

A VINEYARD KEEPER.

WHILE the strong sun in fierceness shines,
    While rains beat heavily,
    She works amongst the Master's vines,
        Their faithful keeper she;
And her great, loving spirit pines
    That faithful she may be.

"Child, well dost thou thy tasks fulfil
    In service fair and fit,
With zeal, devotion, knowledge, skill,
    All graces aptly knit;—
But thy own vineyard on the hill,
    How doth it fare with it?

"Dost thou not e'er in noontide heat
    Thy tears of anguish weep,
Because that hillside vineyard sweet
    Thou hast no time to keep?
Or, with a cry, half stifled, beat
    The silence, grim and deep?"

She lifted up those holy eyes,
    Where love, that casts out fear,
Shone through their sweet solemnities,
    And answer'd calm and clear,—
No truer voice beyond our skies
    Falls on the Father's ear:—

"Did not my Lord, the day His grave,
  Sweet presence bow'd my soul,
Gather me in His arms and crave
  As He had made me whole,
I would go forth for Him who gave
  His life to pain and dole?

" Did He not say, with that intense
  Look of His bent on me,
'Child, thou shalt tend thy vines from hence
  Duly and faithfully;
In quietness and confidence
  Knowing thy strength shall be?'

"And tell me, if I watch and pray,
  My labour shall be bless'd;
His vines put forth new fruit each day,
  Whence shall His wine be press'd;
And I shall deeply know alway,
  In this true labour, rest?"

"But, gentle one, dost thou not fear
  The wild beasts of the wood?"
"They may not fright me; here, just here,
  His feet, nail-piercèd stood:
They dare not venture wheresoe'er
  There is that track of blood."

"Dost thou not fear the winter wind,
  The vines should crash and toss,
And mar thy work with breath unkind?"
  "Nay, love shall save their loss,

K

And drooping branches safely bind
    To their true stay, a cross."

"And when my Master's vines upraise
    Their clusters deepening red,
O'er my own vineyard sweet always
    The showers of peace are shed;
Who watereth for Him, He says,
    Shall thus be waterèd."

"Dost thou not weary, far from Him
    With whom thou fain wouldst be?"
"Yea, but in shadow, sweet though dim,
    His lovely face I see;
And o'er the sea of sounds doth swim
    His lovely voice to me.

"He holds me, will not let me go,
    Lest I should swerve or miss;
His lips with all love's glory glow,
    Once stung by traitor kiss;
And leaning on His heart, I know
    Him mine, as I am His."

"And when thy work is done?" "Oh nay!
    He will not bid me cease,
But breathe on me, that so I may
    Do His sweet will and please;
From strength to strength brought every day
    In His own time of peace."

EDEN.

HOW often in despairing mood
    I summon up the mournful past
    And gaze upon it, till at last
I lose all sense of any good !

How often have I sung in vain
    The dirges of the empty years,
    And sought with self-bewailing tears
To blunt the edge of cruel pain !

How oft comes back the bitter sense
    Of utter lifelong loneliness,
    And lack of anything to bless
My love with equal recompense !

How often in the frozen night
    In weary wakefulness I lie,
    And with th' exceeding bitter cry
Against my condemnation fight !

A sick child crying in the dark,
    And stretching helpless arms of love,
    More desolate than that one dove
That cross'd the waste from out the Ark.

"Like song-birds in their prison-cage,
  Shut in betwixt the earth and sky
  We cannot live, we may not die;
So rolls the world from age to age.

"We blindly strive against our fate,
  We roam the globe from pole to pole,
  We cannot find one kindred soul,
Or if we find, we find too late!

"Such mirage as our life can show
  Amidst a howling desert lies;
  The brazen glitter of the skies
But mocks the misery below."

"Ungrateful fool," the voice replies,
  The hidden voice that dwells within,
  "It is not sorrow, it is sin
By which thy wounded spirit dies.

"Since Adam's time the sons of men
  Have ranged the planet all about,
  And thought to find their Eden out,
And dwell in Paradise again;

"And knew not that the primal curse
  Which shut the Garden of Delight,
  Had blinded all their inner sight,
And made them see the better, worse.

Eden.

"For each one's Eden lies around
   The spot of earth he calls his home;
   He has not any need to roam,
Tho' thorns and thistles choke the ground.

"He needs but simple faith and grace
   To purge the scales from off his eyes;
   Then may he see the Paradise,
And know it for his native place.

"There falleth freely all abroad
   The 'hidden manna' from above;
   There flows the rich, strong wine of love,
'The chalice of the grapes of God.'[1]

"And there the lonely-hearted sees
   Sweet angel forms on either hand;
   His guardian saints around him stand,
Or walk beneath the garden-trees."

"As sometimes in a dream men gain
   Short glimpses thro' an open'd door—
   Within, the loved ones gone before,
In softest blaze of glory reign.

"So in the kingdom of the cross,
   The earthly garden of delight,
   Walk human angel forms of light
To cheer us through defeat and loss."

[1] "In Memoriam."

Therefore, tho' I be weak and sad,
  I will forbear my craven tears,
  I will not weep for blighted years,
I may with heaven's joy be glad.

For, streaming far upon my life,
  The glory of the cross is thrown,
  And angel voices widely blown
Speak peace above the inner strife.

The Chrism-cross upon my brow,
  The spirit-sword within my hand,
  I go to join God's warrior-band,
And take His sacramental vow.

REV. R. WINTERBOTHAM.

A CAROL FOR CHRISTMAS EVE.

NIGHT deepens o'er a woman in woman's sorest need,—
Faint, wayworn, soil'd with travel, seeking where God would lead;
She pauses at a portal where many enter in,
And there are warmth and food, and laughter's merry din.

There are voices loud and angry, and rude unholy mirth,
And rich men richly feasting on good things of this earth;
But the humble, mean-clad Mary, no room for her was there,
So she turn'd her from them meekly into the chill night air.

Outcast, despised, unheeded, none caring for her fate,
That helpless woman turns her from the unfriendly gate.
And is there, then, no refuge in this her hour of woe?
The skies are dark above her, the bitter night-winds blow.

Hath the cold world no shelter for one "o'er women
    blest?"
For thee, O highly favour'd, earth hath no place of
    rest,
Save where the herd is gather'd in yonder stable shed,
And there the patient Virgin lays down her weary
    head.

'Twas silence when the temple rose noiseless from
    the ground,
And silence here is brooding o'er mystery profound;
A voice—an Infant's wailing, from that poor manger
    stall,—
The Voice whose awful thunder unto the dead shall
    call!

Night's gloom is o'er the pastures—o'er the herdmen
    keeping ward;
Lo! brightness in the heavens! the glory of the Lord!
Then heard they gracious anthems bidding them
    fear no more,
Strange accents, all unearthly, from heaven good
    tidings bore.

They sang of man forgiven, of God's eternal love,
Of Christ from heaven descending, that man might
    dwell above;
Upon the world's deep darkness had shone the
    Light of God,—
The tender plant had budded, Jesse's undying Rod.

    *   *   *   *   *

A Carol for Christmas Eve.

A voice within the temple—the high priest watcheth
 there;
Deep in its holy places he pours his soul in prayer;
The lamps are dimly burning where the priest kneels
 to pray,
Shedding a faint pale splendour upon his locks of
 gray.

Perchance the old man museth on that "house" of
 gems and gold
Rear'd by the son of David in the far days of old;
Perchance he thought, in sadness, of Zion's primal
 light,
Of miracle and symbol, strange words, and deeds of
 might.

Alas! no arm of terror strikes for Judæa now;
The ashes of affliction are scatter'd o'er her brow;
Proud Rome's far-flying eagle o'ershades her with
 his wing;—
Beneath that baneful shadow what buds of hope
 may spring?

The times are changed and evil, the glory hath
 grown dim,—
The mantle of his fathers had fallen not on him.
Messiah! why dost Thou tarry? why ling'rest Thou
 so long?
Why com'st Thou not to rescue the captive from the
 strong?

A Carol for Christmas Eve.

If, in that night's deep darkness, such thoughts within him sprung,
Oh, deeper far, and darker, the veil that o'er him hung!
He reck'd not of the Dawning by prophets seen afar,—
He knew not It had risen—the only guiding Star.

He watch'd not for the advent of the meek, lowly Child,
The eternal Priest, unchanging, the Harmless, Undefiled.
Thus suddenly, in silence, Thou cam'st, Lord, to Thine own,
And dull eyes fail'd to know Thee, and Israel's heart was stone.

Alas! we may not blame them, nor vaunt our keener sight,
Who know, but will not love Thee,—believe, but not aright.
Saviour! in all around us, each good or evil sign,
In Thy servants' holy patience, when the world mocks at Thine,

In words of peace and blessing, received on bended knee,
In that deep fount of quiet, the will bow'd down to Thee,
And at Thy holy altar, in deep contrition's sigh,
In joys of pardon'd spirits,—Lord, may we feel Thee nigh!

F. M. H.

AUTUMN.

So still—so still! Only the endless sighing
    Of sad Æolian harp-notes overhead!—
Only the soft mass-music for the dying!
    Only the requiem for the newly dead.

So strangely dim!—the grey mist on the heather,
    The chill cloud-twilight in the wind-stripp'd bowers,
Where gold and scarlet sunlights lay together
    On harvest fruit and summer wealth of flowers!

So empty now!—only the dead leaves sifting
    The dead brown berries underneath the trees;
Only my fair dead treasures idly drifting
    About my footsteps in the autumn breeze.

All over now! No flowers that must be tended
    Are left to grow upon the open plain;
No fruits to ripen: for the harvest's ended!
    There's no more need for either sun or rain.

The infinite hope—the boundless, strong endeavour—
    The love and joy I never thought to sum—
The precious things that were to last for ever—
    All gather'd now, and nothing more to come.

Autumn.

Only the shroud of snow—the white star-tapers—
    The passionate storm-winds, wailing in the air;
Only the icy rain and tearful vapours—
    Only the winter-darkness of despair!

      *   *   *   *   *

So still—so sweet! with tender breezes blowing
    Amongst the hills and o'er the lowland sod,
And golden drifts of dead leaves softly strowing
    The seed-graves, hollow'd by the hands of God.

So grey and calm! the crimson glory faded
    From this low sky, pale blue and purple-barr'd—
This placid sea, with steel and silver shaded—
    This fair earth, now with autumn furrows scarr'd.

And beauty still in all the landscape blending—
    The beauty born of faith, and hope, and rest;
As in a saintly life when near the ending,
    When all its strife and labour has been blest.

The harvest time is past. But there remaineth
    The well-stored treasure-house—the hidden seed
That dead leaves help to nourish, which containeth
    The germ and promise of true life indeed.

ADA CAMBRIDGE.

OUR FATHER IN HEAVEN.

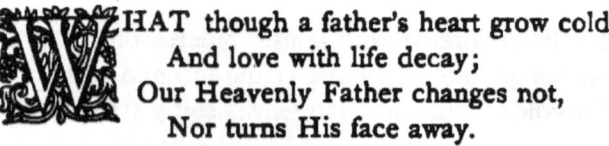HAT though a father's heart grow cold,
    And love with life decay;
Our Heavenly Father changes not,
    Nor turns His face away.

And though a mother's long-tried love
    Forget the son she bore,
Not such the Love which, all unloved,
    Loves on for evermore.

O! not from us, but from our sins,
    God turns away His face;
Even the very prodigals
    He takes to His embrace.

Is He our Father, and are we
    So fallen, of heavenly birth?
Yes, for eternal love has bridged
    All between Heaven and earth.

Sin made the breach, but God destroy'd
    The gulf which none could span,
When men became the sons of God,
    And God the Son of Man.

Our Father, so then not alone
  We lift our prayer on high;
All Christians at the Throne of Grace
  Raise that one common cry.

Our Father, then, as we love Him
  We love who with us call;
Not few, at best most selfishly,
  But all, as He loves all.

Love still must win the world to God,
  To all things true and good;
The banner over us is love—
  Love, badge of brotherhood.

This Love of God is God Himself,
  Our Father throned above;
For He whom God Incarnate loved,
  Saith, children, God is Love.

Then, when we love, we seem like Him;
  Nor is this all our boast:
He dwells in us, and we in Him,
  Most, when we love Him most.

Our hearts a dwelling-place for God!
  The mind sinks down oppress'd
At thought of having Heaven within,
  Our Father for our Guest.

We sound the depth of ocean's caves,
  We soar in upper air;
Science puts out her hands to God,
  And Work seems well-nigh Prayer.

We gird the earth with bands of thought,
  We stay the lightning's flight;
Is man to be Omnipotent,
  Or mortal Infinite?

No! for this earth, with all her pride,
  Breaks down dismay'd, o'er-awed,
Before the thought no mortal grasps,—
  God, and the Love of God.

WM. CHATTERTON DIX.

THE FELLED TREE.

TREMBLING shadows, scatter'd gleams
of glory,
Where the summer sunlight falls and
breaks
Over wrinkled roots and branches hoary,
Dropping here and there in golden flakes.

Diamond dews upon the hawthorns twinkle,
Merle and mavis pipe their mellow lay;
And like fairy chimes the sheep-bells tinkle
Faintly from the pastures far away.

Low it lies—the stately forest giant,
Stretch'd upon the ferns and grasses sweet;
All the winter long it stood defiant
Of the bitter blast and driving sleet.

All the winter long it bore the burden
Of the frozen snowflakes chill and white;
Waiting calmly for the summer's guerdon,
Dancing leaves, soft wind, and golden light.

Wild March breezes sang and whistled loudly,
April smiled and wept her silver tears,
Bright May blossom'd,—and the tree stood proudly,
Robed in "living green," among its peers.

The Felled Tree.

June's blue heaven shone upon her roses,
    Larks trill'd high above the growing corn;
One sweet day in song and perfume closes,
    And the tree lies low at early morn.

Smitten by the axe, and cleft asunder
    In the gladness of a summer hour;
Did it bear the storm and brave the thunder,
    Thus to perish in its day of power?

Better thus to die than live forgotten;
    Better fall while trunk and limbs are sound,
Than endure for ages sear'd and rotten,
    As a cumberer of God's fair ground.

Not in pity of thy fallen beauty
    Should we mourn for thee, O forest friend!
May our lives like thine be strong in duty,
    May we make, like thee, a noble end.

                    SARAH DOUDNEY.

By permission from "The Leisure Hour."

"HE WILL REST IN HIS LOVE."

"HE will rest in His love," for His love is unchanging,
  No tempest shall move it, no cloud dim its light;
He will rest in His love, for that love was from ever,
  Before a star shone on the bosom of night.

"He will rest in His love," for His truth and his mercy
  Were knit by the Saviour in lasting embrace;
So He who was pledged in His justice to punish,
  Now justifies those that believe in His grace.

"He will rest in His love!" hast thou sinned, art thou fearing,
  His patience is wearied, His favour is gone?
Thy God, ere He chose thee, foreknew all thy weakness,
  And loving thee once, will for ever love on.

"He will rest in His love" when the friends I have cherish'd
  Have left me forsaken, in sorrow to weep;
Some parted by distance, some faithless and changing,
  And some in the grave, where I laid them to sleep.

" He will rest in His love."

And O, when the light of my life is declining,
  When heart and flesh fail me, His arm from above
Will comfort my spirit, will guide me, and lead me
  Far out of the shadows to rest in His love.

REV. H. L. NICHOLSON.

THE WRECK OF THE "ROYAL CHARTER."

WHO that ever for his heart's relieving
    Went to natural things for sympathy,
Told the wild woods of his spirit's grieving,
    Sang his sorrows to the moaning sea,

But hath chidden, with a vain appealing,
    Those great trees that stood so fair and still,
Flowers that bloom'd on without care or feeling,
    Motionless lake and calmly purple hill?

Ah! that vast, impassive, heartless Nature
    Hath no ear for any human sob,
Not the warm blood of a sentient creature,
    Not the pulse that gives back throb for throb.

Chide her not—a silence more mysterious,
    And a darkness that thou canst not scan
Hang around thee, in thy pride imperious,—
    O, the strange unconsciousness of man!

He the fond, the earnest, ever making
    Golden links to bind him to his kind,
Smiles on, while those links afar are breaking,
    Ignorant of snow-drift and of wind.

How we watch'd those fair spring eves and morrows,
    On to genial June from surly March,
Careless saw the young corn green the furrows,
    And the red sheath dropping from the larch.

Pluck'd the white thorn, and the gorse flowers yellow,—
    All the time along their hopeless way,
One by one, dropp'd down each gallant fellow
    Frozen in that cruel Arctic May.

We lay sleeping calmly and incurious
    When the east wind swept that wild Welsh cliff,
Or look'd out and said, "The storm grows furious,
    Now God help the seaman in his skiff;"

Heard the arras shake upon the panel,
    Heard the wind howl round the curtain'd room,
While the great ship labour'd in the channel,
    Struck and parted with one shriek of doom.

Island Mother, was it well to greet them,
    Home-sick wanderers straining for thy strand?
Hadst thou in thy cruel hand to meet them,
    But the ribb'd rock and the foam-dash'd sand?

For those giant forests, ever showing
    Changeless green above their fields of brown,
They have felt Old England's breezes blowing,
    They have seen her ports of old renown.

Every time they hear the cordage rattle
  She draws nigh—they all sank in her sight,
As a victor dies in his last battle,
  As a young bride on her marriage night.

White frock'd diggers from those quarries golden,
  Laden with the nuggets of their toil;
Gentle souls that recollections olden
  Turn'd to seek again their native soil.

Treasures of red dust in iron cases,
  All the priceless treasures of man's home,
Women's tender hearts, and children's faces—
  Bore that good ship o'er the green sea foam:

Laugh'd to scorn the wild Pacific weather,
  Spurn'd the winds—and went down with one shock:
Father, mother, children, lie together
  In the surf by Moelfra's cruel rock.

Men will come and talk with one another,
  They will raise the gold dust from the sand,
Father, mother, sister, child, and brother,
  Never, never shall they come to land.

That vile thing for which man gives his Heaven,
  Lies unhurt beneath the whelming wave,
But the gift divine that God has given,
  One short struggle, and what arm can save!

Life—that subtle godlike flame that dieth
    In a moment, but shall never die,—
Hundred-voiced from out that wreck she crieth,
    And the gurgling whirlpool makes reply.

In thy pride, O man, give answer never
    To that last shriek of their parting breath—
Leave them in that Hand that holdeth ever
    The strange issues of our life and death.

He, perchance, upon the threshold met them,
    Yearning for that home that lay before,
In a higher Heavenly home He set them,
    Where no ships go down along the shore.

Sing their requiem, mother, child, and peasant,
    They lie still beneath that rock-bound main,
Hoping, praying, judge not of their present,
    For ye know not of their parting pain.

C. F. A<small>LEXANDER</small>.

NOT NOW.

"He that had been possessed with the devil, prayed him that he might be with Him."—St. Mark v. 13.

NOT now, my child,—a little more rough tossing—
A little longer on the billows' foam—
A few more journeyings in the desert-darkness,
And then the sunshine of thy Father's Home!

Not now,—for I have wand'rers in the distance,
And thou must call them in with patient love;
Not now,—for I have sheep upon the mountains,
And thou must follow them where'er they rove.

Not now,—for I have loved ones sad and weary—
Wilt thou not cheer them with a kindly smile?
Sick ones, who need thee in their lonely sorrow—
Wilt thou not tend them yet a little while?

Not now,—for wounded hearts are sorely bleeding,
And thou must teach those widow'd hearts to sing;
Not now,—for orphan's tears are thickly falling—
They must be gather'd 'neath some sheltering wing.

Not Now.

Not now,—for many a hungry one is pining—
   Thy willing hand must be outstretch'd and free;
Thy Father hears the mighty cry of anguish,
   And gives His answering messages to thee.

Not now,—for dungeon walls look stern and gloomy,
   And pris'ners' sighs sound strangely on the breeze—
Man's pris'ners, but thy Saviour's noble freemen;
   Hast thou no ministry of love for these?

Not now,—for hell's eternal gulf is yawning,
   And souls are perishing in hopeless sin;
Jerusalem's bright gates are standing open—
   Go to the banish'd ones, and fetch them in!

Go with the name of Jesus to the dying,
   And speak that Name in all its living power;
Why should thy fainting heart grow chill and weary?
   Canst thou not watch with me one little hour?

One little hour!—and then the glorious crowning—
   The golden harp-strings and the victor's palm—
One little hour!—and then the Alleluia!—
   Eternity's long, deep, thanksgiving psalm!

C. P.

WHAT THEN?

WHAT then? Why then another pilgrim song;
  And then, a hush of rest, divinely granted;
And then, a thirsty stage; (ah, me, so long!)
  And then, a brook just where it most is wanted.

What then? The pitching of the evening tent;
  And then, perchance, a pillow rough and thorny;
And then, some sweet and tender message, sent
  To cheer the faint one for to-morrow's journey.

What then? The wailing of the midnight wind;
  A feverish sleep; a heart oppressed and aching;
And then, a little water-cruse to find
  Close by my pillow, ready for my waking

What then? I am not careful to inquire;
  I know there will be tears, and fears, and sorrows;
And then a loving Saviour drawing nigher,
  And saying, "I will answer for the morrow."

What then? For all my sins His pardoning grace;
  For all my wants and woes, His lovingkindness;
For darkest shades, the shining of God's face,
  And Christ's own hand to lead me in my blindness.

What Then?

What then? A shadowy valley, lone and dim;
  And then, a deep and darkly rolling river;
And then, a flood of light—a seraph's hymn,
  And God's own smile, for ever and for ever.

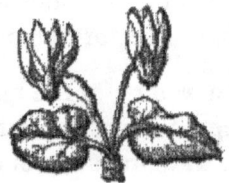

UNREST.

WHY thus longing, thus for ever sighing,
    For the far off, unattain'd and dim,
While the beautiful, all round thee lying,
    Offers up its low, perpetual hymn?

Wouldst thou listen to its gentle teaching,
    All thy restless yearnings it would still;
Leaf and flower and laden bee are preaching,
    Thine own sphere, though humble, first to fill.

Poor indeed thou must be, if around thee
    Thou no ray of light and joy canst throw;
If no silken cord of love hath bound thee
    To some little world through weal and woe:

If no dear eyes thy fond love can brighten,
    No fond voices answer to thine own;
If no brother's sorrow thou canst lighten,
    By daily sympathy and gentle tone.

Not by actions that the crowd applauses,
    Not by works that give the world renown,
Not by martyrdom, or vaunted crosses,
    Canst thou win and wear the immortal crown.

Daily struggling, though unknown and lonely,
    Every day a rich reward will give;
Thou wilt find, by hearty striving only,
    And truly loving, thou canst truly live.

REST IN GOD.

UNDER the shadow of Thy wings, my Father,
   'Till these calamities be overpast!
In that sure refuge let my spirit gather
   Strength to look calmly back upon the past.

Be merciful to me! for thoughts that crush me
   Lie like a weight of sorrow on my breast;
Only Thy voice, Omnipotent, can hush me
   Into the quiet e'en of seeming rest.

Thou knowest—Thou only—the dark chain that binds me,
   The heavy chain which eats into my soul;
The links of adamant which have entwined me,
   Binding each feeling in their chill control.

Oh! what is life but one long, long endurance
   Of this dull, heavy weight on heart and brain?
Speak to my spirit—speak the strong assurance
   That nothing Thou ordainest is in vain.

Trembling amid the turmoils of existence,
   Oh! let me grasp a more than mortal arm;
Father! my Father! be not at a distance
   When earth's dark phantoms Thy weak child alarm.

Rest in God.

Under Thy shadow! Fear cannot appal me
  If in the Rock of Ages surely hid;
Under thy shadow! Harm cannot befal me
  If Thou,—All wise! All-merciful!—forbid.

Nearer to Thee!—my Saviour! my Redeemer!
  In earth, or heaven, whom hath my soul but Thee?
Though for an instant, as some feverish dreamer
  Grasps at the treasures which he seems to see,

I, too, have dreamed, and waked to find "illusion"
  Inscribed on all I sought to make my own;
And turning from my idols in confusion,
  I dedicate my life to Thee alone.

Under the shadow of Thy wing abiding,
  Close to a sympathizing Saviour's side,
In the sure promise of His love confiding,
  Why should I shrink, though earthly ills betide?

Oh! if the soul grew strong through suffering only,
  If but through trial it may reach its goal,
I will rejoice, although my way be lonely,
  And all Thy waves and billows o'er me roll.

Yes! I will praise Thee! though my tears are falling
  Upon the trembling harp-string as I sing;
Am I not safe—though grief my soul is thralling—
  Under the shadow of my Father's wing?

R. A. R

EVENING HYMN.

THE shadows of the evening hours
    Fall from the darkening sky;
  Upon the fragrance of the flowers
    The dews of evening lie:
Before thy throne, O Lord of Heaven,
    We kneel at close of day;
Look on thy children from on high,
    And hear us while we pray.

The sorrows of thy servants, Lord,
    O do not thou despise;
But let the incense of our prayers
    Before thy mercy rise;
The brightness of the coming night
    Upon the darkness rolls:
With hopes of future glory chase
    The shadows on our souls.

Slowly the rays of daylight fade;
    So fade within our heart
The hopes in earthly love and joy,
    That one by one depart:
Slowly the bright stars, one by one,
    Within the heavens shine;—
Give us, O Lord, fresh hopes in Heaven,
    And trust in things divine.

Evening Hymn.

Let peace, O Lord, thy peace, O God,
   Upon our souls descend:
From midnight fears and perils, Thou
   Our trembling hearts defend;
Give us a respite from our toil,
   Calm and subdue our woes;
Through the long day we suffer, Lord,
   O give us now repose!

A. A. PROCTER.

VESPERS.

SHADOW in a sultry land !
We gather to thy breast,
Whose love, unfolding like the night,
Brings quietude and rest,
Glimpse of the fairer life to be,
In foretaste here possess'd !

From aimless wanderings we come,
From drifting to and fro ;
The wave of being mingles deep,
Amid its ebb and flow,
The grander sweep of tides serene
Our spirits yearn to know !

That which the garish day had lost
The twilight vigil brings,
While softlier the vesper bell
Its silver cadence rings,—
The sense of an immortal trust,
The brush of angel wings !

Drop down behind the solemn hills,
O Day, with golden skies !
Serene above its fading glow,
Night, starry-crown'd, arise !
So beautiful may Heaven be,
When Life's last sunbeam dies !

C. M. P.

HEAVEN.

BEYOND these chilling winds and gloomy
　　skies,—
　　Beyond death's cloudy portal,—
　There is a land where beauty never dies,
And love becomes immortal,—

A land whose light is never dimm'd by shade,
　　Whose fields are ever vernal,
Where nothing beautiful can ever fade,
　　But blooms for aye eternal.

We may not know how sweet its balmy air,
　　How bright and fair its flowers;
We may not hear the songs that echo there,
　　Through those enchanted bowers.

The City's shining towers we may not see
　　With our dim earthly vision;
For death, the silent warder, keeps the key
　　That opes these gates Elysian.

But sometimes, when adown the western sky
　　The fiery sunset lingers,
Its golden gates swing inward noiselessly,
　　Unlocked by silent fingers.

Heaven.

And while they stand a moment half ajar,
    Gleams from the inner glory
Stream brightly through the azure vault afar,
    And half reveal the story.

O land unknown! O land of love divine!
    Father all wise, eternal,
Guide, guide these wandering, way-worn feet of mine
    Into those pastures vernal.

                      N. A. W. Priest.

"NO MORE SEA."

(Rev. xxi. 1.)

"AND there was no more sea."
    Oh blot in brightness set!
    Among the promised future joys
Must there be one regret?
Must the new earth's fair landscape want
    The broad main rolling free,
With waves which catch the sun aslant?
And we must miss their tuneful chant,
    In that new age
    When there is no more sea?

Our hearts delight to dream,
    The pure new earth and heaven
Will show that nature's loveliness
    Was not to perish given;—
That still the beauty of the flowers,
    The glory of the tree,
The golden light of summer hours,
In other forms will deck their bowers:
    Yet will be loss,
    If there is no more sea!

No boundless blue expanse,
    Where waves range line on line,

"No more Sea."

Crown'd, then discrown'd, with golden crowns,
    That shine and fall and shine ;—
No bracing breath on breast and brow
    Of sea-breeze breathing free ;—
No pearl or shell from depths below ;—
No mirror for the sunset's glow :—
      No more of these,
    When there is no more sea !

    O sea ! O glorious sea !
      Thou brightest in thy mirth !
Thou grandest in thy raging wrath !
      Thou majesty of earth !
Will Earth her glorious things recall,
      And find no room for thee,
The oldest glory of them all ?
Must thou into oblivion fall,
      While they smile on,
    Where there is no more sea ?

    O sea ! O solemn sea !
      How have I loved thee here,
E'en for the mystery, vastness, depth,
      Which blends our love with fear.
How wistfully in yon fair scene
      Mine eyes will strain for thee,
Across the landscape, too serene,
The fields and groves of fadeless green,—
      If such appear
    Where there is no more sea !

So plain'd my doubting heart;
  I bowed my head and wept;
And whispering wavelets to my feet,
  In mournful answer crept:
Yet, mid their murmurs of farewell,
  There came a voice to me,
Which seem'd in tender tones to tell
My listening spirit it was well
    That after this
    There should be no more sea.

It said, " Yon wild sea strives
    To pass its lawful bound;
And though the mightiest wave it sends
    Is forced to kiss the ground,—
It gathers up its force once more,
    To conquer and be free,—
And rushes madly on the shore,
And still falls baffled as before.
    But peace will reign
    Where there is no more sea.

" In moaning restlessness
    It tosseth night and day,
Changeless in change,—while ages roll,
    And nations pass away.
Upon its breast the stillest star
    Must ever broken be;
And would it not that glory mar,
Which shines so calm in heaven afar,
    And shall on earth,
    When there is no more sea?

" Have not yon wailing waves,
    Which thrill thee with their sound,
Within thy soul some vague response,
    Some answering murmur found?
Has not thy heart with their unrest
    Too deep a sympathy?
Lies not their spell within thy breast?
But wails would find in spirits blest
    No echo there,
    Where there is no more sea.

" No wild self-lashing force,
    Furious yet impotent,—
No dreary grey and weary waste,—
    No ceaseless long lament,—
No rush and roar 'neath tempests' frown,—
    No ships in agony,—
No wrecks, no cries of them who drown,—
No corpses settling fathoms down;—
    No more of these,
    When there is no more sea !

" But once a heaven-taught seer
    Beheld a sea of glass,
Upholding feet; whereon and through,
    Did fiery splendour pass.
Bright crowns of gold, down bowing, told
    God's Spirit there breathed free;
And songs like many waters rolled,
Songs which shall cease not when unfold
    The gates of pearl,
    When there is no more sea.

"No more Sea."

"Too bounded and too dim,
　　A mirror true to be,
You sea gives yet an image faint
　　Of deep eternity.
And more sublime stupendousness,
　　Profounder mystery,
Unsetting glories that impress
More light on breadths more measureless,
　　Thou'lt find in God,
　Where there is no more sea!"

C. F. M.

WAITING BY THE GATE.

BESIDE a massive gateway built up in
  years gone by,
 Upon whose top the clouds in eternal
  shadow lie,
While streams the evening sunshine on quiet wood
  and lea,
I stand and calmly wait till the hinges turn for me.

The tree-tops faintly rustle beneath the breeze's
  flight,
A soft and soothing sound, yet it whispers of the
  night;
I hear the wood-thrush piping one mellow descant
  more,
And scent the flowers that blow when the heat of
  day is o'er.

Behold the portals open, and o'er the threshold,
  now,
There steps a weary one with a pale and furrow'd
  brow;
His count of years is full, his allotted task is wrought;
He passes to his rest from a place that needs him
  not.

In sadness then I ponder how quickly fleets the hour
Of human strength and action, man's courage and his power.
I muse while still the woodthrush sings down the golden day,
And as I look and listen the sadness wears away.

Again the hinges turn, and a youth, departing, throws
A look of longing backward, and sorrowfully goes;
A blooming maid, unbinding the roses from her hair,
Moves mournfully away from amidst the young and fair.

Oh glory of our race that so suddenly decays!
Oh crimson flush of morning that darkens as we gaze!
Oh breath of summer blossoms that on the restless air
Scatters a moment's sweetness and flies we know not where!

I grieve for life's bright promise, just shown and then withdrawn;
But still the sun shines round me: the evening bird sings on,
And I again am soothed, and, beside the ancient gate,
In this soft evening sunlight, I calmly stand and wait.

Waiting by the Gate.

Once more the gates are opened; an infant group
    goes out,
The sweet smile quench'd for ever, and still'd the
    sprightly shout.
Oh frail, frail tree of Life, that upon the green sward
    strows
Its fair young buds unopened, with every wind that
    blows!

So come from every region, so enter, side by side,
The strong and faint of spirit, the meek and men of
    pride.
Steps of earth's great and mighty, between those
    pillars gray,
And prints of little feet, mark the dust along the
    way.

And some approach the threshold whose looks are
    blank with fear,
And some whose temples brighten with joy in
    drawing near,
As if they saw dear faces, and caught the gracious eye
Of Him the Sinless Teacher, who came for us to die.

I mark the joy, the terror; yet these, within my heart,
Can neither wake the dread nor the longing to depart,
And in the sunshine streaming on quiet wood and
    lea,
I stand and calmly wait till the hinges turn for me.

          WILLIAM CULLEN BRYANT.

SUNDAY EVENING.

ANOTHER Sabbath sun is down,
  Grey twilight creeps o'er thorp and
      town.
    How much of sorrow unconfess'd
Lies hidden in yon darkening west!

What burdens, uncomplaining borne!
What masks o'er latent anguish worn!
What pangs of heart-break! plots of sin!
Have this night's shadows folded in!

We woke to-day with anthems sweet
To sing before the mercy-seat,
And, ere the darkness round us fell,
We bade the grateful vespers swell.

Whate'er has risen from heart sincere,
Each upward glance of filial fear,
Each litany, devoutly pray'd,
Each gift upon Thine altar laid;

Each tear, regretful of the past,
Each longing o'er the future cast,
Each brave resolve,—each spoken vow,—
Jesus, our Lord! accept them now.

Whate'er beneath Thy searching eyes,
Has wrought to spoil our sacrifice;
Aught of presumption, over bold,
The dross we vainly brought for gold;

If we have knelt at alien shrine,
Or insincerely bow'd at Thine,
Or basely offer'd "blind and lame,"
Or blush'd beneath unholy shame;

Or,—craven prophets,—turned to flee
When duty bade us speak for Thee;
Mid this sweet stillness, while we bow,
Jesus, our Lord! forgive us now.

Oh, let each following Sabbath yield
For our loved work an ampler field,
A sturdier hatred of the wrong,
A stronger purpose to grow strong;—

And teach us erring souls to win,
And "hide" their "multitude of sin;"
To tread in Christ's long-suffering way,
And grow more like Him day by day.

So as our Sabbaths hasten past,
And rounding years bring nigh the last;
When sinks the sun behind the hill,
When all the "weary wheels" stand still;

Sunday Evening.

When by our bed the loved ones weep,
And death-dews o'er the forehead creep,
And vain is help or hope from men ;—
Jesus, our Lord! receive us then.

W. M. P<small>UNSHON</small>.

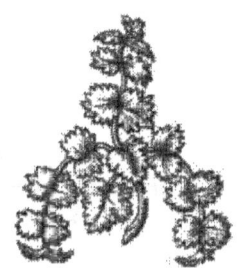

TWILIGHT.

O dim and cold and lonely—with no light
   Of golden sunset, or of sweet moonrise,
   To stir the broad grey shadow as it
      lies
About my bed and on my heart to-night.

All is in darkness.   In the little room
   Where I am lying, restless and in pain,
   I look for the familiar things in vain—
My books and pictures—they are lost in gloom.

And so I feel the twilight in my heart,
   Blotting out darkly the familiar things,
   The old sweet joys and fair imaginings,
Wresting my life and its bright dream apart!

So dim and lonely.   The dumb sense of wrong,
   The vacant wishes that lie dead and cold,
   The hopes that promised never to grow old,
The broken faith that had been built so strong—

I think of this, and fling my arms above
   My hot head in the darkness; and I think
   The chalice all too bitter now to drink
Which was so sweet with the old trustful love!

Twilight.

A streak of daylight glimmers through the night,
    And, like a warning finger, tries to trace
    The dim, sweet outlines of a holy Face,
Of Hands and Feet nail-piercèd—marble white!

The long black bars—crossing upon the wall,
    The carven Figure of the thorn-crown'd King,
    Whose tender pity aye is fathoming
The sorrows of His children—healing all!

Why should I care that books and pictures lie
    Deep in the darkness, since mine eyes can fix
    My thoughts upon that sacred Crucifix—
Upon the light and love that cannot die?

Why should my heart of hope be dispossess'd,
    Mourning for sunny day-dreams blotted out?
    The gloomy shadows, lying round about,
Leave the one vision where its eyes would rest.

                    ADA CAMBRIDGE

NIGHT AND MORNING.

PEACEFUL were the plains that night,
    Where the sheep lay sleeping;
Stars shone out, like flowers of light,
    In the Angels' keeping:
Things seem'd as they ever were,
    Since the fathers slumber'd—
Suddenly, the cohort fair,
    Multitude unnumber'd.

What the tidings that they brought
    To the royal nation?
Wonder, which the Lord had wrought
    Through the Incarnation:
This they told, that God was born
    Of the Mother-maiden;
Therefore leap the sad this morn,
    Rest the heavy-laden.

Clouds and darkness hie away,
    Light o'er earth is breaking,
Since the old law's sunset-ray
    Died last night, forsaking
Temple, sacrifice, and rite
    Of the ancient letter;
Old things past, the Lord of Might
    Brings us new and better.

Yesterday for thee, poor world,
　But to-day for Jesus:
Pride and scorning down are hurl'd,
　'Tis a Babe Who frees us.
Dreary years of waiting past,
　Now is come salvation,
Peace, Goodwill, and, wrought at last,
　Reconciliation.

W. C. Dix.

THE THORN IN THE FLESH.

EACH pang I feel is known to thee,
　　Dear Lord! for thou hast sent the thorn
　　　　That pierceth me;
Hast fix'd it festering in this breast,
That with new anguish wakes each morn,
　　　　And finds no rest.

Though oft with burning tears I've pray'd
That thou wouldst take this grief away,
　　　　Thou hast delay'd;
Yet thou hast pledged thy word to keep,
To succour in the sorrowing day
　　　　Thine own who weep.

Why tarriest thou? Long must I plead,
With hope deferr'd, that thou wilt send
　　　　The help I need?
Hast thou thy words of love forgot,
That when, o'erwhelm'd, I lowly bend,
　　　　Thou answerest not?

Be still, my soul, and meekly bear
Thy pain, nor yield one doubt a place,
　　　　Lest dark despair
Prevail, thy stedfast trust to shake;
Though in thick shades He hides his face,
　　　　The dawn shall break!

Ah! now, at last He speaks;—a thrill
Sweeps through my soul, and tides of love
    My being fill :—
" Canst thou not bear the cross with Me?
I may not yet the thorn remove
    That woundeth thee;—

But thou shalt lean upon My breast,
My strength shall make thy weakness strong ;
    When most oppress'd,
Then most My grace shalt thou partake ;
And from thy burden'd heart a song
    Of joy shall break !"

RAY PALMER.

THE BLOOD OF SPRINKLING.

BLOOD of sprinkling! healing tide,
   Life and peace bestowing;
From its fount in Jesus' side,
   Full and ever-flowing:
Like the stream in Horeb, struck
From the cleft and living rock,
On it flows, and flows for me,
Ever near and ever free.

Heart of Jesus! pierced for me,
   Pledge of sins forgiven;
Mirror'd in Thy fount I see
   All the smiles of heaven.
Thence, when sin has stung my soul,
Flows the balm that makes it whole,
Life to God, and death to sin,
Peace without, and peace within.

Every rival I dethrone,
   Every tie dissever;
Lamb of God! reign thou alone
   In my heart for ever.
Wash it clean from every stain,
Cool its fever, soothe its pain,
Chase its gloom, and clear its way
Onward to the perfect day.

J. GUTHRIE.

"IN THE FATHER'S HOUSE."

THE wanderer no more will roam,
The lost one to the fold has come,
The prodigal is welcomed home,
    O Lamb of God, in Thee!

Though clad in rags, by sin defiled,
The Father hath embraced His child;
And I am pardon'd, reconciled,
    O Lamb of God, in Thee!

It is the Father's joy to bless;
His love provides for me a dress,
A robe of spotless righteousness,
    O Lamb of God, in Thee!

Now shall my famish'd soul be fed;
A feast of love for me is spread;
I feed upon the children's Bread,
    O Lamb of God, in Thee!

Yea, in the fulness of His grace
He puts me in the children's place,
Where I may gaze upon His face,
    O Lamb of God, in Thee!

"In the Father's House."

I cannot half His love express,
Yet, Lord, with joy my lips confess
This blessèd portion I possess,
    O Lamb of God, in Thee!

It is Thy precious Name I bear,
It is Thy spotless robe I wear;
Therefore the Father's love I share,
    O Lamb of God, in Thee!

And when I in Thy likeness shine,
The glory and the praise be Thine,
That everlasting joy is mine,
    O Lamb of God, in Thee!

IN THE CHURCHYARD.

 YE dead! O ye dead! you are lying at
your rest;
I am lying just above you, and I know
not which is best;
Just between us are the grasses, and the gravel,
and the clay,
But they measure not the distance into which you
pass away.

Reaching downward grow the rootlets of the flowers
and the heath;
But they cannot touch the bodies that are lying
underneath—
For the eye and ear have wasted, and the busy
heart decay'd—
Dust to dust you're all resolving, as from dust you
all were made.

I look upon the sunshine and the sea-waves as they
roll,
And the clouds in high mid-heaven — are such
sights before your soul?
I hear the breeze and streamlet, and the curlew
and the sheep
Bleating far upon the mountain—do they wake you
out of sleep?

In the Churchyard.

Do you know the change of seasons, as of old they come and go—
Now the flowers, now the fruitage, now the fading, now the snow?
Do you feel a sudden trembling when the loved ones tread above,
And the echo of their footsteps is the echo of their love?

Do you find a thrill of sorrow, as the husband or the wife
Dry their tears for the departed, and begin to search their life—
Till another takes his station in the fields you used to tread,
And another takes your pillow, and upon it lays her head?

Do such earthly matters move you? You are pass'd from hence away,
Into larger joys and sorrows than belong to this our day;
And you look down on the whirling of this life with calmer eyes,
That have learnt to bear the measure of Eternity's surprise.

Are you near us? can you see us? Can you watch us in our ways?
Do you witness all the evil, all the good of all our days?

Do you, knowing all things better, wonder at us in
    our strife,
As we clutch the tinsel gilding, and pass by the
    Crown of Life?

O ye dead! O ye dead! young and old, and small
    and great,
Now you know your doom of sorrow, or your high
    and blest estate,
And I wonder as I ponder, what you feel and what
    you see;
As according to the sowing, so your reaping now
    must be.

O ye dead! O ye dead! small and great, and young
    and old,
I am longing for your secret, and my longing makes
    me bold—
But since the day they brought you from your
    houses on the hill,
You have kept your secret stedfast, and I know
    will keep it still.

"HE KNOWETH OUR FRAME."

WHAT can we do, o'er whom the unbeholden
   Hangs in a night with which we cannot cope?
What but look sunward, and, with faces golden,
   Speak to each other softly of a hope?

Can it be true, the grace He is declaring?
   Oh, let us trust Him, for His words are fair!
Man, what is this, and why art thou despairing?
   God shall forgive thee all but thy despair.

Truly He cannot, after such assurance,
   Truly He cannot and He shall not fail;
Nay, they are known, the hours of thine endurance,
   Daily thy tears are added to the tale.

Never a sigh of passion or of pity,
   Never a wail for weakness or for wrong,
Has not its archive in the angels' city,
   Finds not its echo in the endless song.

Not as one blind and deaf to our beseeching;
   Neither forgetful that we are but dust;
Not as from heavens too high for our up-reaching,
   Coldly sublime, intolerably just;—

"He Knoweth our Frame."

Nay, but Thou knewest us, Lord Christ, Thou
    knowest ;
  Well Thou rememberest our feeble frame ;
Thou canst conceive our highest and our lowest
    Pulses of nobleness and aches of shame !

Therefore have pity !—not that we accuse Thee,
    Curse Thee, and die, and charge Thee with our
    woe :
Not through Thy fault, O Holy One, we lose Thee,—
    Nay, but our own,—yet hast Thou made us so !

Then though our foul and limitless transgression
    Grows with our growing, with our breath began,
Raise Thou the arms of endless intercession,
    Jesus, divinest when Thou most art man !

FREDERIC W. H. MYERS.

WAITING FOR JESUS.

"JESUS, I wait." Last words breathed soft and low
 From dying lips grown tremulous and faint:
O great Life-giver, Thou didst surely know
 The yearnings of Thy Saint.

Waiting—a moment only—just a pause,
 A hush before the music had begun;
A silence ere the cloudy veil withdraws,
 And the bright Home is won.

"Jesus, I wait." Was He not waiting too,
 With hands outstretch'd in welcome and with eyes
Brimful of love, to guide His servant through
 The gates of Paradise?

O calm safe rest; all sorrows pass'd away
 Like twilight mists before a risen moon;
O blessèd close to life's most weary day,
 O peace, attain'd so soon!

Teach us to live, and living, wait for Thee,
 Redeemer,—making life and labour sweet;
Watching and working till our eyes shall see
 The Face they long to greet.

Our highest earthly bliss, to do Thy will;
  Our hope, the promise of Thy great reward;
Our effort, all Thy purpose to fulfil,
  And magnify the Lord.

Teach us to wait,—as waits the ripen'd corn
  In golden fulness for the reaper's hand;
Meet for Thy garner, when the harvest morn
  Dawns o'er the weary land.

And Thou wilt come with radiant angel train,
  Lord of the harvest, claiming all Thine own.
Then shall we greet our dearest ones again,
  And know as we are known.

Then shall the endless Festival begin,
  And the long waiting as a dream go past;
For love, triumphant over death and sin,
  Shall reign supreme at last.

SARAH DOUDNEY.

AMERICAN MISSIONS.

LORD, when Thou didst come from Heaven,
   Edom sought Thee, from afar,
     With her gold and incense given,
  By the leading of a star;
Westward then, from Eden guiding,
  Was the light of Bethlehem shed;
Like the pillar'd blaze abiding
  O'er the wandering Hebrew's head.

Westward still, the world alluring,
  Hath the risen Day-Star beam'd,
And, the sinking soul assuring,
  O'er the world's wide ocean stream'd.
Westward still, the midnight breaking,
  Westward still its light be pour'd!
Heathen thy possession making,
  Utmost lands, Thy dwelling, Lord!

Westward, where from giant fountains,
  Oregon comes down in flood.
Westward to Missouri's mountains,
  Or to wild Iowa's wood;
Where the broad Arkansas goeth,
  Winding o'er savannahs wide,
Where, beyond old Huron, floweth
  Many a strong eternal tide.

Westward, where the wavy prairie
   Dark as slumbering ocean lies,
Let Thy starlight, Son of Mary,
   O'er the shadow'd billows rise!
There be heard, ye herald voices,
   Till the Lord His glory shows,
And the lonely place rejoices,
   With the bloom of Sharon's rose.

Where the wilderness is lying,
   And the trees of ages nod,
Westward, in the desert crying,
   Make a highway for our God:
Westward—till the Church be kneeling
   In the forest aisles so dim,
And the wildwood's arches pealing,
   With the people's holy hymn!

Westward, still, oh Lord, in glory
   Be Thy banner'd cross unfurl'd,
Till from vale to mountain hoary,
   Rolls the anthem round the world;
Reign, oh reign o'er every nation,
   Reign, Redeemer, Father, King,
And with songs of thy salvation
   Let the wide creation ring!

          A. C. COXE, *Bishop of Western
          New York.*

IN LAVINGTON CHURCHYARD.

(*August* 18, 1873.)

HERE in this quiet spot, so calm and blest,
    Where flowers gleam bright and early sunbeams smile,
'Twas meeter far He should be laid to rest
    Than in the grand old Minster's solemn aisle.

Here, 'neath the shadow of the Church's cross,
    Beside the dear ones whom he loved so well,
Yes, here he sweetly sleeps. But O the loss
    To those still left behind, what words may tell!

How strange it seems! Beneath this quiet mound
    All that is mortal of the great Man lies;
Those marvellous lips in solemn silence bound,
    And closed for ever those deep, speechful eyes!

O great Heart! All thy throbbings still'd at last;
    O busy hands! Claspt coldly on thy breast;
O noble brow! All care and suffering past,
    The life-toil over, ye have won your rest.

In Lavington Churchyard.

O quiet grave! Cross-crown'd and bright with flowers,
  How eloquent thy pleading voice to me;
He is not dead: his teaching still is ours;
  His works "shall follow" through the years to be.

Rest from thy labours, Shepherd of the sheep,
  Thy Pastoral staff laid in a moment down;
Thy "course is finish'd," thou the Faith didst keep,
  And thou shalt wear for aye the Master's crown.

R. H. BAYNES.

INDEX OF FIRST LINES.

	Page
GAIN, O Lord! Thy Church the song is swelling	116
Ah, Lord! to be	23
A Lamb is dead! . . .	78
And doth thy last deep longing yet remain . .	98
"And there was no more sea"	164
And thus our hearts appeal to them . . .	26
Another Sabbath sun is down	172
At work within his barn since very early .	124
Before the dawn has streaked the skies . .	66
Beside a massive gateway built up in years gone by	169
Beyond these chilling winds and gloomy skies .	162
Blood of sprinkling! healing tide . . .	181
Dead but a moment! and my Daughter's kiss .	48
Each pang I feel is known to Thee . . .	179
Hath He who reaps the wheat and leaves the tares	120
He will rest in his love for his love is unchanging	146
Here do I wait to greet	106
Here in this quiet spot, so calm and blest . .	193

	Page
Hills of heaven, bright and shining	15
How often in despairing mood	131
How thin the veil between our eyes	8
"I am the Resurrection and the Life"	111
I dream'd a dream, while piping low	31
I would go home,—home to my Father's dwelling	73
It is the night; the lights are burning low	5
"Jesus, I wait;" last words breathed soft and low	189
Jesus, thou true and living Bread	46
Keep we the feast, with solemn joy, too holy	87
"Let Thy Will be done!" One prayed	39
Light the lamps, 'tis eventide	12
Lo, if a man should hear, all night, in dreaming	1
Lord, from this time we cry to thee	37
Lord! in love and mercy save us	29
Lord, when Thou didst come from Heaven	191
Lost are the years gone by? We hold them still	118
Mid darkest haunts of sin	59
My Father! God of life and light	75
Night deepens o'er a woman in woman's sorest need	135
Not now, my child,—a little more rough tossing	152
O beautiful, comforting words	41
O hands outstretch'd for me	77
O Michael, bright archangel, calmly standing	82
O shadow in a sultry land!	161
O ye dead! O ye dead! you are lying at your rest	184

Index of First Lines.

	Page
Of all the lovely seven	93
Oh, Christ, my God! to Thee I once arose	36
Oh, spear-torn heart, dear place to hide	43
Over moor and over mere	114
Peaceful were the plains that night	177
Perchance it is an idle thought	127
Ring out the bells from Dudley's ancient tower	70
Saviour, comest Thou to me	122
Sepulchred and wave-wash'd dead	55
"She is not dead!"	14
So dim and cold and lonely—with no light	175
So still—so still! Only the endless sighing	139
Sure, on no fairer, sweeter spot than this	85
Thank God that Gerizim's sweet dews have	62
The shadows of the evening hours	159
The wanderer no more will roam	182
They are going—ever going—through this pilgrim land below	50
They look'd towards the west	71
Thou hast cross'd the troubled waters	89
Thou, who on Calvary's tree	44
Thron'd on a sea of gold, upheaves a cluster of columns	101
Trembling shadows, scatter'd gleams of glory	144
Under the shadow of Thy wings, my Father	157
We come to Thee, sweet Saviour, humbly seeking	21

Index of First Lines.

	Page
"We have eaten in Thy presence; Thou hast taught within our streets"	80
We praise Thee, God our Father . . .	91
We whisper, "It is over now for thee" . .	19
What can we do, o'er whom the unbeholden .	187
What is life, but sowing	57
What then? Why then another pilgrim song .	154
What though a father's heart grow cold . .	141
When the clouds loom dark and eerie . .	17
While the strong sun in fierceness shines . .	128
When thy virgins' lamps are burning . . .	108
Who that ever for his heart's relieving . .	148
Why thus longing, thus for ever sighing . .	157
Why weepest thou?—to Mary Magdalen . .	53
Ye whose hearts with grief and sin are dreary .	104

THE END.

CHISWICK PRESS:—C. WHITTINGHAM, TOOKS COURT,
CHANCERY LANE.

Works by the Rev. H. R. Haweis, M.A.

CURRENT COIN. Materialism—The Devil—Crime—Drunkenness—Pauperism—Emotion—Recreation—The Sabbath. Crown 8vo., price 6s.

SPEECH IN SEASON. Third Edition. Crown 8vo., price 9s.

THOUGHTS FOR THE TIMES. Ninth Edition. Crown 8vo., price 7s. 6d.

UNSECTARIAN FAMILY PRAYERS for Morning and Evening for a Week. With short selected passages from the Bible. Square crown 8vo., price 3s. 6d.

Works by Mark Evans.

THE GOSPEL OF HOME LIFE. Crown 8vo. [*Preparing.*

THE STORY OF OUR FATHER'S LOVE, told to Children. Being a New and Enlarged Edition of Theology for Children. With Four Illustrations. Fcp. 8vo., price 3s. 6d.

A BOOK OF COMMON PRAYER AND WORSHIP FOR HOUSEHOLD USE. Compiled exclusively from the Holy Scriptures. Fcp. 8vo., price 2s. 6d.

Works by the Rev. Samuel Davidson, D.D., LL.D.

THE NEW TESTAMENT, translated from the Latest Greek Text of Tischendorf. A New and thoroughly revised Edition. Post 8vo., price 10s. 6d.

CANON OF THE BIBLE: its Formation, History, and Fluctuations. Second Edition. Small crown 8vo., price 5s.

THE LIFE AND WORDS OF CHRIST. By Cunningham Geikie, D.D. With Map. Two vols., 4to., bevelled boards, price 30s.

PRAYERS, WITH A DISCOURSE ON PRAYER. By George Dawson, M.A. Edited by his Wife. Crown 8vo., price 6s.

WOMANHOOD: its Duties, Temptations, and Privileges. By Rev. Joseph Shillito. A Book for Young Women. Crown 8vo., price 3s. 6d.

Henry S. King and Co., London.

WORKS BY THE LATE REV. F. W. ROBERTSON, M.A., OF BRIGHTON.

NOTES ON GENESIS. New Edition. Crown 8vo., price 5s.

EXPOSITORY LECTURES ON ST. PAUL'S EPISTLES TO THE CORINTHIANS. A New Edition. Small crown 8vo., price 5s.

LECTURES AND ADDRESSES, with other literary remains. A New Edition. Crown 8vo., price 5s.

AN ANALYSIS OF MR. TENNYSON'S "IN MEMORIAM." (Dedicated by Permission to the Poet-Laureate.) Fcp. 8vo., price 2s.

THE EDUCATION OF THE HUMAN RACE. Translated from the German of Gotthold Ephraim Lessing. Fcp. 8vo., price 2s. 6d.

SERMONS. Four Series. Small crown 8vo., price 3s. 6d.

The above Works can also be had bound in half-morocco.

*** A Portrait of the late Rev. F. W. Robertson, mounted for framing, can be had, price 2s. 6d.

WORKS BY THE REV. STOPFORD A. BROOKE, M.A., Chaplain in Ordinary to Her Majesty the Queen, and Minister of Bedford Chapel, Bloomsbury.

THE LATE REV. F. W. ROBERTSON, M.A., Life and Letters of. Edited by.

    I. Uniform with the Sermons. 2 vols. With Steel Portrait Price 7s. 6d.

    II. Library Edition. 8vo. With Two Steel Portraits. Price 12s.

    III. A Popular Edition. In 1 vol., 8vo., price 6s.

THE FIGHT OF FAITH. A New Volume of Sermons. Crown 8vo., price 7s. 6d.

THEOLOGY IN THE ENGLISH POETS. Cowper, Coleridge, Wordsworth, and Burns. Third Edition. Post 8vo., price 9s.

CHRIST IN MODERN LIFE. Ninth Edition. Crown 8vo., price 7s. 6d.

SERMONS. First Series. Ninth Edition. Crown 8vo., price 6s.

SERMONS. Second Series. Third Edition. Crown 8vo., price 7s.

FREDERICK DENISON MAURICE, The Life and Work of. A Memorial Sermon. Crown 8vo., sewed, price 1s.

HENRY S. KING AND CO., LONDON.

www.ingramcontent.com/pod-product-compliance
Lightning Source LLC
Chambersburg PA
CBHW020828230426
43666CB00007B/1140